THE BRUSSELS CRISIS

VERSAILLES-WEIMAR EFFECT

Cacildo Marques

2nd edition

Copyright © 2018 Cacildo Marques
All rights reserved.

ISBN: **978-1986038874**

Cover illustration: Cacildo Marques

Marques, Cacildo
The Brussels Crisis/ Cacildo Marques. Maryland. EpistemeEd , 2018.

124p.
ISBN: 978-1986038874

1. Global Financial Crisis – Social features. 2. World Economy – Social features. 3. Finance – Wold Economical Politics – Political Sociology. 4. Economic History - 21st Century I. Titles   CDD 338.542

Second edition, 2018.

Based in the first edition published in Sao Paulo, Brazil, in 2012.

CONTENTS

	Introduction	1
0	The Versailles-Effect and the fall of Rome	2
1	China: the birth of the paper money	15
2	The geocentric vision of the monetarism	24
3	The Brazilization of South America	32
4	The reason of the civilizing mission of Europe	57
5	The repair in the education	80
6	Paths for the European Union	104

The Brussels Crisis

Cacildo Marques

THE GREATEST HYPERINFLATION IN THE HISTORY

In the following picture it is the essence of the model, about the importance of the capitals. Casual coincidence? Let's to think, because the world is not a magic.

Country	Daily rate	Chief of State
Hungary 1946 July	195.4%	Lake Balaton
Zimbabwe 2006 Nov	98.0%	Borrowdale Brook
Yugoslavia 1994 Jan	64.6%	Itinerant capital
Germany 1923 Oct	20.9%	Weimar
Greece 1944 Nov	17.1%	Crete
China 1949 May	13.4%	Nanjing

Source: Prof. Steve H. Hanke, February 5, 2009 (Cato Institute).

Preface to the Second Edition

Some punctual corrections and need to specify better some words have led me to the decision to publish this second edition of this book, originally released in 2012, the year it was written.

Its central thesis is that, for my surprise, the installation of capital in a consolidated city as national capital other than the main capital of the bloc could trigger the problems of the Versailles-Weimar Effect, of monetary misconduct, as well as in cases where one takes the residence of the chief of State to a city without a historical status of capital (by the way, I came to call Ravenna Effect the Versailles-Weimar Effect phenomenon).

Since the European Union has succeeded, with much effort and sacrifice, in overcoming its crisis, and apparently without tricks that stifle the inflationary impulse of the Ravenna Effect, as Brazil did in 1994, a new conclusion must be made explicit here in this preface: to install the residence of the chief of State in capital that is not the principal, but which has a historical status of national capital, triggers economic crisis, but does not claim the 120 years of consolidation that new cities, such as Washington, or old and without historical status, such as Madrid and Tokyo, demanded, leaving behind them a brutal trail of blood from wars, migrations, and impoverishment.

I urge the reader to bet on the validity of the above assertion, so that a new European Union crisis caused by its capital Brussels will not be returned.

Another issue that needs to be discussed here is that the notion that a perpetual or long-term ruler is an harmful institution to human life has not yet been understood as scientific, and this needs to be done urgently, because figures such as Evo Morales and Xi Jinping find great support of its political bases to impose their project of eternal dictatorship.

Hitler was not disastrous as a lifetime ruler because he was a bad man, but because he was an energetic life-long chief. The same must be said of Francisco Franco, Ferdinando Marcos, Nicolae Ceausescu,

Enver Hodxa, Josef Stalin, and how many more have sat in the chief's chair to no longer leave while they were alive. The exceptions, the lifetime rulers who did not cause tragedy, were spiritless people, mere puppets.

The illusion that there is no science behind the conclusion about the pathologicity of the lifelongness of the ruler comes from the fact that is not yet consolidated the idea that Psychology is one of the hard sciences. Well, the basic hard sciences, of laboratory, are: Mathematics, Astronomy, Physics, Chemistry, Biology, Ethology and Psychology. The latter has three noble areas that are subsidiary to it: Psychosociology, Semiology and Psycholinguistics.

Psychology, yes, is hard science, and it guarantees that life-long ruler represents social tragedy. In respect to Russia, which has changed from four to six years with a re-election the size of its presidential term, we must consider this period, 12 years, as the current tolerable limit. In the medium term, we must work to bring the limit to two consecutive five-year terms, and, in the longer period, two terms of 2.5 years, as it is currently in the European Union.

Even those who doubt the result about the tragedy must bear in mind that, from the fifth year onwards as the head of a country, the individual will be deciphered by his subordinates, being no longer able to exercise power by the mystery emanating from his person, having to act, from there, either as a fool or as a tyrant, or a mixture of the two, not to be defenestrated.

Cacildo Marques, Sao Paulo, February 2018

THE BRUSSELS CRISIS

VERSAILLES-WEIMAR EFFECT

Cacildo Marques

Manneken Pis – monument in Brussels

THE BRUSSELS CRISIS: VERSAILLES-WEIMAR EFFECT

Introduction

We know that a scientific model is valid for sake of its forecast capacity. When the reproduction of an experiment leads to a previously delineated result, without manipulation or improper interferences, we have the confirmation of the assertive that gives base to the discovery. The proof's denial of this relationship of cause and effect, in any instant of the events, represents the refutation of the theory and with this a lot of hypotheses are discarded everyday in the world of the science, be by the formulator ones themselves, be by the peers who are assigned of doing the requested tests.

The "second fall of Rome" was a forecast announced few years before the financial crisis that reached the euro, the common currency of the most of the countries in the European Union. Some European authorities were alerted that such would happen, but maybe they have not understood the foundation of the warning. Therefore a new book is written now on the theme, with all of the possible subsidies to the understanding of the phenomenon. If they continue shooting outside of the target, it won't be because of the lack of knowledge of the problem, but by reasons much more humans, in the sense of the weakness that makes us bearers of the unconscious evil.

At the beginning, it is necessary a summary of the model and of the foundations that accompany it, for then we proceed to a more detailed explanation of the theme.

In the text, the question that tops each item is just a way of clarifying more the idea of the subtitle, and the entire book can be read without it, which is not part of the concatenation of the themes.

0. The Versailles-Weimar Effect and the Fall of Rome

A new, or secondary, capital is the cause of the economical disasters.

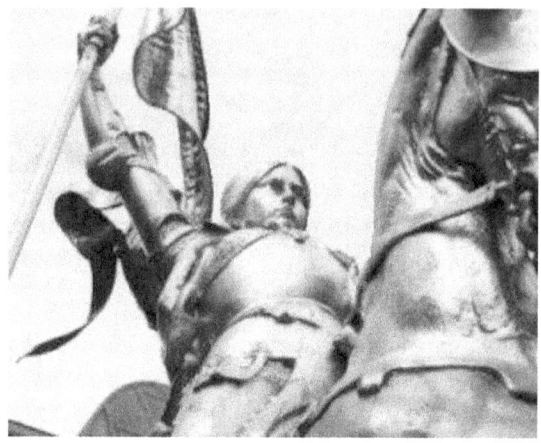

Joan Of Arc: martyrdom by the retaking of Paris

Name. What name is more appropriate for us to refer to this fact?

The phenomenon, identified firstly in 1975, was called Versailles Effect, and, soon then, Versailles-Weimar Effect, once other researchers already were using the first name with several meanings. Lately, the expression Versailles-Weimar Effect lives together with another more simple, which can come to substitute it: Ravenna Effect. Versailles-Weimar[1] is, however, more explanatory name, because it joins an artificial city, which caused serious political-economical problems, and a city already old, but that didn't have the weight requested to accomplish the role that was attributed to it when, for misfortune of German, entered the history.

Operation. How does it happen the working of the phenomenon?

Before everything that was observed already, the Versailles-Weimar Effect is characterized by the following occurrences. (A) A person doesn't govern alone, nor even in absolutist regime; one governs with his court, and the enlarged court is the city. (B) The city that serves as model of behavior to the country is not the city of the prime minister, but, yes, the one of the chief of State. (C) The residence of the chief of State needs to be a city with secular status of capital. (D) Chief of State living in capital without secular status leads to the Versailles-Weimar Effect, or Ravenna Effect, the destructive pulse upon the symbols, mainly on the currency of the country. (E) Versailles-Weimar Effect's action doesn't limit itself to the country under jurisdiction of the chief of State in question, but it influences neighbors States that are subsidiary of the capital without status. (F) In a given country, the capital without secular status, the noxious capital, is one that is alternative to the traditional capital. (G) The secular capital needs to have more than a hundred years as residence of the chief of the national State. (H) In a union of States, the capital with secular status cannot be a secondary capital; on the contrary, it has to be one of the main capitals. (I) If one settles new capital in city without secular status, the destructive Versailles-Weimar Effect will last approximately 120 years, until the city acquires the status. (J) Versailles-Weimar Effect's action on the currency provokes disarray in the inflation, interests and exchange rates, and, if there are efficient mechanisms of combat against the inflation, the country cannot escape from living together with pathologies of exchange or interests. (K) Under the Effect, the inflation can be tamed, but not the inflationary pulse, which will bring headaches to the authorities by a lot of decades, because the financial cost of the control is very high. (L) Versailles-Weimar Effect's by-products are debts, coup d'état, revolutions, civil wars, international wars, deindustrialization, bad education, impoverishment and diaspora. (M) The expectation of the inhabitants of the country under capital without status is that the courtiers come to be upstarts - since the ones of the traditional capital are abandoned, - and the behavior upstart becomes the model. (N) A new man (an upstart chief) in capital with status secular cause harm incomparably smaller than a chief originated from the traditional rich society living in capital without status. (O) A new artificial capital is necessarily a capital without status (Versailles), but a capital installed in old city that have not been principal capital during at least one century

(Weimar) causes equivalent damage. (P) Also a traditional capital inside of a block provokes Versailles-Weimar Effect if it is a secondary capital (Sarajevo) containing the chief of State's residence. (Q) A capital with secular status that stops being the chief of State's residence loses its status after one century.

Center. And which is the central fact in all of those occurrences?

The summary of the whole opera is: the chief of State settles in capital without secular status, city that is neither the main nor the traditional capital of the country, or of the Union, and the whole population under his jurisdiction starts to have as model of behavior the upstarts' action, that join around him, in his new city. The contempt to the symbols - currency, railways, grammar, ethics and so on - characterizes the Versailles-Weimar Effect. Once the traditional elites, that sustain the value of the symbols, they are changed by upstarts, the population, in a general way, starts to act in agreement with the model of this new class. All of the difficulties, losses and tragedies observed under the Versailles-Weimar Effect they result of this psychosocial phenomenon.

Genesis. How did the perception of this fact grow?

As stated above, the first perception on the effects of the new capital happened in 1975, having as observation object the city of Brasilia. A small text, under the hegemony of the new middle class, hegemony favored by the recent capital, was elaborated, and was incorporated to the first book published on the theme, in 1988, with title "Brasilia: capital of the bonanza?". The text treated of the typical habits of the new class and of how this new class arose as model of conduct to the country. In the thirteen years elapsed between this first text and the publication of the book, it grew the perception of the influence of this behavior on the pathologies of the currency.

Enigma. Is the prime minister's residence free of blame, or does it only matter the chief of State's house?

After eighteen years elapsed of this approach of 1975, a big mystery was solved, when then, as a consequence of that explanation, the book "Ten ways to abolish the inflation" was published, in September 1993.

That book was written along a trip to the historical cities of the State of Minas Gerais in the month of July of that same year. What was deciphered then was what one called after "Enigma of Berlin", the explanation of because the Federal Republic of Germany, said Occidental Germany, it had, in every year of its existence, the administrative capital in the city of Bonn, which centuries ago had stopped working as capital, and even like this it didn't present symptoms of the Versailles-Weimar Effect. It was noticed that the Versailles-Weimar Effect doesn't depend on government's leadership, but on the leadership of State, in a way that the administrative capital in Bonn didn't produce any negative effect on Germany, once the presidential residence was always in Berlin, the traditional capital. The observation of the situation of India, not the one of Germany, is what made possible to solve the "Enigma", because the capital New Delhi doesn't lodge the presidential residence, which stayed in Delhi. India presents many economical problems, but not the one of the inflationary pulse, even with the administrative capital in new city. The reading of the book "The new industrial State" (1967), of John Kenneth Galbraith, is what sharpened this perception.

Abstraction. How did Versailles-Weimar Effect's observation lead to the creation of the abstract currency?

The book "Ten ways to abolish the inflation" presented an invention that already the following month it was used and this today seems old thing. The European Union itself used it in the release of the euro. It is the abstract currency, the scriptural money that has a value, but that doesn't have a printed form, be metallic, be foliar. Such currency is used in the contracts, in the payments and in the electronic transactions, but, not possessing form physics, of paper or metal, it is immune to the inflation. As every intellectual creation, the invention of the abstract currency didn't appear of the nothing, but it came from an elaboration about the distinction done by Mario Henrique Simonsen between printed money and scriptural money. The abstract currency answers to the three characteristics of the currency: unit of account, reservation of value (in bank account form) and medium of exchange (via the scriptural registrations or the electronic transference). In this way, also the three reasons for its retention (precautionary, transactional and speculative) continue valid.

Thread. How does it settle down a connection among the historical situations due to the phenomenon?

The following chronology is part of a manifesto written to the Brazilian Senate. Ravenna of Honorius and Romulus Augustulus needed 74 years (from 402 to 476 BC) to give the Roman Empire to the barbarians of Odoacer; Madrid, city for which Felipe II moved in 1561, it provoked immediately a period of a lot of decades of monetary disarray - with beginning already registered in book by Jean Bodin in the year 1568, denominated in 1934 as "Price Revolution", by Earl J. Hamilton -, passing by the Portuguese Restoration War, in 1640, and then the domain of the planet was transferred from Spain to Great Britain; Washington, 1800, was set on fire by English in 1812 and it was rebuilt, and in 1861, 61 years after having been installed, it was refuted by a part of the United States, in favor of the city of Richmond, in the War of Secession that it provoked; Versailles needed 107 years to lead the Parisian ones to conduct to the Storming of the Bastille, rioted with a brutal increase in the price of the bread; Tokyo became capital in 1869, already provoking in the beginning of the 20th century great diaspora and leading Japan to the war against China in 1937 (68 years after becoming capital), and against the United States in 1941 (72 years as capital); in the recent years the world accompanies the Versailles-Weimar Effect in Myanmar, under dictatorship of military, who transferred its capital, and in the Republic of Nigeria, with its new capital Abuja, since 1991, which still didn't provoke great misfortunes besides the more than ten thousand died in ethnic conflicts in several points of the country; Ankara, capital of Turkey since 1923 (it lacks a little to consolidate itself), disputes with Brasilia since many years ago the first place in discharge of interests, after having been also liberated of a long military regime. Before the Versailles-Weimar Effect one didn't obtain a conductive thread between the silver of Potosi (1561) and the wages of the valley of Ruhr (1919).

Gap. Why there are just few registrations on the role of the national capitals?

One of the reasons of the difficulty for reaching the result presented here is the fact that the historians were always concerned with the chronicle of the countries and their rulers, giving little importance to the role of the capitals of those countries. Rome is one of the few exceptions, since all of the roads led to Rome; nevertheless, the expression "fall of the Roman Empire" is more usual than "fall of Rome", and it is almost a secret of academy the fact that the "fall of the Roman Empire" happened when Ravenna, and not Rome, was the capital. It was during a lecture of the model's author to students of a university, in 1994, that it appeared the idea that in the year 476 the Roman Emperor didn't live in Rome, because, otherwise, the theory would not have a lot of validity. Soon after the lecture, a fast research revealed Ravenna as residence of the chief of State of the Roman Empire. The case of Versailles is more difficult of hiding, because it is central part of the events that generated the French Revolution. But, also in this case, the negligence is well-known: it is known that the Palace of Versailles was built by Louis XIV and that it was used by Louis XV and by Louis XVI, but any parallel line is not built among the intensification of the permanence of the monarchs in this house and the political and economical events of France, the city getting known, distant twenty kilometers of Paris, just as headquarters of the scandals of the court after the entrance of Marie Antoinette in the French political scenery. Weimar, as one knows, had its name associated to the German super inflation from 1919 to 1923, simply because one gave to the political period the name of "Republic of Weimar", a nickname highly providential, but whose light shone without being seen until the last decade of the 20th century.

Difficulty. Why is so difficult to convince the people of the validity of the theory?

People are prisoner of paradigms that impede the vision of the arrival of the new vehicle. An intellectual who accompanied the most of the development of the concept has taken long ten years for believing in the Versailles-Weimar Effect. For the most ones, the results of the Psychology do not make sense, and the relationship between Economics and Social Psychology seems manipulation. More than this, for the least clairvoyants, the facts that influence the economy of a country are purely economical facts, never political, psychological or ethological ones. Economists, historians and politicians still look for, hopelessly, an explanation for the increase of the price of the bread in France on July 13, 1789, for the Japanese diaspora after 1869, for the hyperinflation of Weimar in 1919 and for the conquest of the power in China by the revolutionaries of Mao Tse-Tung in 1949. They see as a curiosity without consequences the fact that the respective chiefs of State, in these cases, didn't live in the traditional capitals of those countries, which should be Paris, Kyoto, Berlin and Beijing. They imagine that, in the same way as some central events of the history happen out of years of end 9, economical disasters can be registered out of the Versailles-Weimar Effect. But this is the same as to think that, given that many persons die of cancer, the heart disease is not death cause, and it should be left of side.

History. Is not the simple division between rich and poor the base of the historical reversions?

The old interpretation of division of classes between rich and poor as basic cause of historical conflict doesn't have factual bearing in the millennia that precede us, nor the modern division between working class and business community justifies the formation of own political parties as John Stuart Mill proposed. The historical materialism looked for sustaining all its philosophical outline in this last dichotomy, but this so much was not solid that it intended the conflict of classes had to be built, being not enough the conscience of "class for itself". That approach has its value, certainly, as part of the evolution of the thought. But the great incompatibility of classes, this yes responsible by the crucial events of 1789, happens among the upstarts, today called members of the new middle class, or emerging class, and the class of the precedent rich, or traditional middle class. Historically, upstarts are absorbed slowly for the ethos of the class of the traditional rich ones, and this process always diluted the latent conflict, except in some specific moments as the one of the fight between Marius and Sulla, which won partisan colors. This immersion of the upstarts' habits in the class of the precedent rich presents many positive episodes in the human history, unlike of what one can imagine. Marcus Aurelius, of traditional lineage, prohibited in the year 176 the introduction of new religions in the Roman Empire, the one that did unchain the cruelest phase of the persecution to the Christians. But Constantine, general who in the year 306 ascended to the power by military merits, man of emerging class, bent to his mother Helena's appeals and, by using the symbol of the cross in the soldiers' shields, he won the Battle of the Milvian Bridge in the year 312, converting himself then to the Christianity, being followed in this by the court and by his subjects, without declaring, however, the Christianity as official religion of the Empire. As everything is not perfect, his great jump in the abyss came in the year 326, after unifying the Empire, when he, without getting escaping of his upstart destiny, adopted Byzantium, which passed to be named Constantinople and, later, Istanbul, as the new capital of the Roman Empire. How an expert and smart military man, he knew how to channel the dissatisfactions come of the new capital for the religious persecutions to the Jews and the heretical ones. The class conflict between rich and poor, finally, doesn't show itself nor even with the ascension of an upstart to the power. The reason of this is that the traditional poor knows that to leave his social condition implicates to change himself in an upstart, of the new middle class, not a rebellious poor. The conflict just turns visible when a new capital is adopted, because then it starts to exist, and, in this case, the upstart doesn't need to be in the top of the hierarchy.

Reverberation. Is not the Versailles-Weimar Effect the key of the history?

The Versailles-Weimar Effect is not the key of the history because one of the more common foundations of the human behavior is the emulation, besides there being still other components. Like this, an effect can happen just because people imitate. For instance, this is the explanation for the fact of South Korea to have adopted the direct presidential election in 1990. It is not a Republic of Cassock, neither Catholic nor Shiite, and, therefore, it doesn't have own psychological reasons to use this politics. The political model was mere copy of the French system, which was implanted in 1848, abandoned by the elected Louis Napoleon in the coup d'état of 1851 and restored by De Gaulle in 1958. In the same way, Italy, which is a Republic of Cassock, comes as exception inside its group, staying in the same presidential model that Germany, maybe by having experimented, with Mussolini, the same demagogic poison that the Germans lived under Hitler (Cuba, the other exception, nobody still knows where it will go; yes, by the Roman side, Vatican has taken measures of correction, as the parish priests mobility, but it needs to go beyond this). Other authors utilized previously the expression "Versailles Effect"[2], without Weimar, to explain the phenomenon of the imitation of a country by other. Countries that were distant of the pre-revolutionary France, as well as many that were close, they followed models of behavior that came from Versailles, as fashion and feeding. Besides the phenomena of the emulation and the deceit, there are other factors that promote the tragedy in the history, as the rulers' lifelongness and the theocratic regime. The key of the history has, therefore, three wings, motivating ones, which are the emulation, the deceit (in the forms of misunderstanding, reverse effect or madness), and the unforeseeable (earthquake, epidemic, and so on), and three feet, causative ones, which are:

(A) the new capital,
(B) the lifelongness,
(C) the theocracy.

Those three feet can appear together or separate, and the most harmful for the economy is the first. For provoking disasters, a foot doesn't need the other, nor the tragedies of the history are all dependents on the economy, but it, when seen damaged, becomes the largest fuel for the revolts that lead to wars, coups d'état and revolutions.

Loud. There is not how the way of life in the new capital to pass unnoticed?

The performance of the capital without status is resounding. Even if, for some miracle, the new capital didn't cause economical-financial problems, the new class formed there has morbid need to show itself. Upstarts forming a hegemonic class do not have as being discreet. Like this, even if they didn't provoke the tragic Versailles-Weimar Effect, they would provoke the Versailles Effect, of the release of new tendencies. They continue in search of new words, new architectures, new garments, new musical styles and new patterns of plastic arts, and those innovations, even not being of good taste, they win the popular preference. The new capital buries as an avalanche the healthy way of life engendered under the influence of the secular capitals.

Hyperinflation. Is there the risk of the hyperinflation return to Europe in full third millennium?

The risk of a developed country, or a monetary union, to develop a hyperinflation today in the level of that of Germany 1919 or of South America of the years 1980 is very small, by the mechanisms that were already developed against this. But those mechanisms, as it was already said, they cool the fever without curing the headache. Once the cost of the continuous anti-inflationary rules is high too much, a lot of social work remains for being done, because substantial volumes of resources are worn-out in commitments as payments of interests or maintenance of the super-appreciated exchange. Everything happens as if money would be made to be burned, which is what the hyperinflation would also do, at the end of all, with the difference that its incinerator work happens under open sky, and the governments appear as criminals of the delinquent action, even when they allow it not by bad faith, but by pure ignorance. In the case of the high interests rates, there is not a Milton Friedman for blaming governments, because the economists are unanimous in putting the blame of this neither in governments nor in banks, but in macroeconomical injunctions that they don't get decipher.

Gift. What aspect of the several discoveries related to the phenomenon is the most auspicious?

The most important point, of all the verifications done after the first perception of the Versailles-Weimar Effect in 1975, was the solution of the Berlin's Enigma. That is because this discovery eliminates the costs of the repair of a great foolishness, which is the installation of the presidential residence in new capital, or in secondary capital. What was seen in 1993 is that it is not necessary to dismount the whole installed base of the administration that has been transferred for certain city, but just to change the chief of State's address, allocating him in the traditional capital, as it was done in India (Delhi) or in Germany (Berlin), or, in the case of a monetary union, settling him in the main capital. This can be made in one only day, being enough a phone call and a trip. The main capital is not, necessarily, the most populous city. Nor it needs to be the richest city. It is, simply, the capital of the State of larger weight, in historical, cultural and political terms. In the case of the European Union, the most populous capitals are London (7,5 million inhabitants), Berlin (3,4 million), Rome (2,5 million) and Paris (2,1 million). They are the capitals of the main States of the block and, like this, one of the four should be the presidential residence of the European Union. As the presidential residence doesn't need to be in State that uses the currency of most of the members, it could be fixed in London. If this is not the case, by some restriction that it come to present, as the fact of being not continental, it can be tried to fasten it in Berlin or Paris, Rome being discarded, once it is already the headquarters of the Catholic Church. Paris was rescued twice in the history as traditional capital: one, by Joan Of Arc, as part of the fight of French liberation in the Hundred Years War; other, by Louis XVI, who yielded to the revolutionaries' appeals. Both ended in martyrdom, although to this second is not attributed any heroism until the current days. With the presidential residence of the European Union in another city, Paris will be without its status of central capital after a hundred years, what will represent the loss of a great patrimony of the humanity. This fact should be considered before making the decision of not testing it as the more appropriate place for the European chief of State's residence.

Trump. What can happen to the monetary union after the cessation of the noxious capital?

It is very important that the chief of State that corrects the problem, installing his residence in the capital with status, resist to the turbulence of the initial days of the change, for more onward to have right to the victory laurels, which it will begin to happen some later weeks, but that will take some years until it is really recognized by everyone. Joan Of Arc, who didn't want the power, but only to serve to the French monarch, whose coronation she militarily sustained, was arrested and immolated under English yoke. Louis XVI decided to flee of Paris, by fear of being condemned, and the escape served as argument to the revolutionaries for condemning him to the death, in such a way that who won the laurels of the economical stabilization was Napoleon Bonaparte, who also took advantage of the Law of the Maximum, or of the maximum price, of the unhappy romantic Maximilien Robespierre, idealizer of the direct election to the presidency. Marshal Hindenburg, President of Germany, from 1925 to 1934, got do little use of the glories of the abandonment of the Republic of Weimar, by having died in the beginning of his second period, so that the credits by the retaking of the economy fell in hands of the premier of the semi-district voting system, Adolf Hitler, vested in 1933 and who, in 1934, proclaimed himself chief of State, as well as Napoleon crowned himself as emperor. In this way, if the chief of State that makes the correct decision of rescuing his healthy capital doesn't have phlegm or luck to resist and then to receive the trumps for the success, the successor will be seen as demigod. If he is not a very prepared statesman, he will use the weakness of the popular good faith for transforming himself in for life dictator, following the example of the Napoleon post-Versailles and the Hitler post-Weimar. It weighs in favor of the marshal Hindenburg the fact of having made everything that was in his scope for avoiding the Nazism: in the parliamentary elections of 1932 the Nazi Party obtained 37% of the chairs for the Parliament, and the President canceled the election, summoning new voting, which Hitler's party was with 32%, that, even so, represented the relative majority, so that Germany didn't have how to escape of the Nazi government, since the semi-district[3] voting system, anti-urban and conservative one, removes the chance of election for the most expressive personalities of the society.

Recovery. How is it possible to notice the transformation of the capital from noxious to healthy?

It is not visible for the observers of the exterior the moment in that a country recovers itself from the Versailles-Weimar Effect, because this happens, in general, in a slow way, step by step, completed the cycle of the harmful influence of the capital, when the city finally consolidates its leading class as traditional establishment. A victim of this deficient reading was Minister Matsuoka, of the foreign relationships of Japan, who, cultivator of great hate against the United States, since the times in that he was an academic student in the west of the country, led the government and the general staff of Japan to deceive the American government and to promote the surprise attack to Pearl Harbor, in 1941, without it was clear the Emperor Hirohito's endorsement to that decision, once his father had been incontestable allied of the United States and Great Britain in the First World War. Without Matsuoka to have become aware, the era of suffering by the noxious capital had been over and now the United States were being driven to win the economical leadership of the world. With some administrative adjustment in the following year, the United States got ready, with France, Great Britain and too much allies, to impose an end - by the western front, since by the oriental front Russia came - to the Hitler's warlike path and his occasion backers, which were Japan and Italy.

(1) *Professor Phillip David Cagan has formulated the concept of Weimar Effect, which simply refer to the people impoverishment provoked by hyperinflation.*

(2) *Professor Malcom Hewitt Wiener, historian, has launched the concept of Versailles Effect, but referring to spreading of fashions, not to economical problems.*

(3) *For being really proportional, the system would have to count on the sixteen German States as electoral circumscriptions, not 35 districts, how it was.*

1. China: the birth of the paper money

The problem of the first paper money came from the loss of the capital Kaifeng.

Zhao Zhen: release of the paper money in 1023

Stores. How did appear the practice of the paper money emission?

Before the 11th century there was not fiduciary currency. The value of the coin corresponded, in theory, to the value of the portion of the metal that it was made with. For high values, the coin had to be of gold; while for medium or small values the silver and other cheaper metals, as copper or brass, were used. It is known, however, that, around the year 1000 AD, in the province of Szechuan, in China, the metals with which the coins were minted were in lack. It was then that the iron became used for this end. That, definitively, was not a good idea, because it was necessary to carry great weights of the metal to do any purchase a little more expensive. Then they created the "money stores", which received those coins as deposit and gave vouchers in paper, with the value of the deposit printed in the document. As the people didn't want to walk carrying weigh thereabout, those paper vouchers were passed forward in the trade and soon they were working as currency. It didn't delay so that many began to abuse of the system, super-appreciating the papers. To solve the problem, in 1023 the government prohibited the operation of the "money stores", and by this time the public authorities had noticed the advantage of issuing that paper money.

Birth. What did government first release the official paper money?

The prohibition didn't mean the end of the service, but just its officialization, because the government itself started to emit the money in paper form, being born then the fiduciary currency and, with it, the history of the inflation. Such fact happened under the Song, or Sung, dynasty, which lasted from 960 to 1279. This is a phase of special relevance in the Chinese history, because it has beginning under the Emperor Taizu of Song - or Zhao Kuangyin, by the name from birth -, with the total unification of China, except the called Sixteen Northern Prefectures, and it closes up with Emperor Zhao Bing (1278-1279), nicknamed posthumously Weiwang, who was dead in the naval battle of Yamen, when Emperor Kublai Khan, from Mongolia, invaded and conquered China, incorporating it to the Yuan dynasty (1271-1368). The Song dynasty is divided in two long periods: Northern Song, from 960 to 1127, and Southern Song, from 1127 to 1279. This division happened when the North was conquered in the invasion of the tartars, by the Jin dynasty (1115-1234), which forced the Song dynasty to just maintain the southern part of the Empire. The successive emperors of the Song dynasty were: Zhao Kuangyin - Taizu (960-976), Zhao Guangyi (976-997), Zhao Heng (997-1022), Zhao Zhen (1022-1063), Zhao Shu (1063 -1067), Zhao Xu - Shenzong (1067-1085), Zhao Xu - Zhezong (1085-1100), Zhao Ji (1100-1125) and Zhao Huan - Qinzong (1126-1127), in the first period; Zhao Gou (1127-1162), Zhao Shen (1162-1189), Zhao Dun (1189-1194), Zhao Kuo (1194-1224), Zhao Yun (1224-1264), Zhao Qi (1264-1274), Zhao Xian (1274-1275), Zhao Shi (1276-1278) and Zhao Bing - Huaizong (1278-1279), in the final period. In this way, the Emperor Zhao Zhen, or Renzong, in the religious name, was the first ruler under whose command the money was printed in paper, on January 12, 1024.

Success. Was right the government's decision of printing paper money in the 11th century?

The historians always interpreted the political and economical facts with the instruments that they had in hands, emphasizing or leaving in second plan situations that seemed to them suitable to such treatments. It was not really possible to take colored photography in the times of Hercules Florence and Daguerre, and they didn't try to do this, differently of the historians, that always wanted to paint the picture in a complete way, even before possessing the necessary technique. Luckily, new discoveries always lead those professionals to review what was said and written before, and nobody feels shame of substituting bad approaches by modern and solid considerations. According to those historiographical weaknesses, the impression that the academy disseminates on the history of the paper money is that a succession of disasters happened, after Zhao Zhen made the decision of closing the "money stores" and concentrating in the hands of the State the incumbency of emitting the valuable paper, called Chiao-Tzu (medium of exchange). This is, for instance, the vision cultivated by Milton Friedman, who, besides, shortens the size of the historical experience. However, it urges to render attention on the dates. Since 1024 to the Mongolian invasion, one century later, China lived under monetary peacefulness. The fact is despised because of the turbulence that has had place. The historians were unanimous in recognizing that China only came to solve its problem of coexistence with the paper money as of 1661, already under the Qing dynasty, and they took the six precedent centuries as a long period of difficult learning, without other earnings that not the lessons of the suffering. But an experience of a first century of success in any invention it casts deep roots. Therefore it is that, in the 20th century, after the great controversies between metallism (the use of the coin of gold) and bimetallism (the use of the coins of gold and silver) in the United States, the era of the paper money finally was consolidated.

Fault. Can an alone chief of State be made responsible by the discharge of the inflation?

For treating the historiography not under the inclination of the magics or of the omens, the historians need to take into account the knowledge on the Ethology and the Social Psychology. Certainly the human factor is important in the political events, but writing down the successive rulers' name and blaming some and exempting other by the bad events, this doesn't bring any plausible explanation for the facts. When the name of Emperor Zhao Gou is associated to the beginning of the inflationary climbing in the Song dynasty, it is necessary to render attention to his address. We needed to do this with Emperor Romulus Augustulus (Ravenna, 476, not Rome), with Louis XVI (Versailles, 1789, not Paris) and Friedrich Ebert (Weimar, 1919, not Berlin). Yes, thanks to the human factor, a man can try to explain the architectural constructions that he saw in Egypt to create with this the geometric demonstrations which are the first scientific results in the history, as Thales of Miletus made it in the 7th century BC; he can discover the arithmetic relationship among the intervals of the musical notes and still to invent an institution for formation of adolescents and young after the literacy, calling it School, as Pythagoras made it in the 6th century BC; he can discover a new regular polyhedron and to demonstrate that only five solids of these species exist, as Plato made it in the 4th century BC; he can invent the display case clock with base in the jagged wheel of Archimedes, as Ctesibius of Alexandria made it around the year 250 BC; he can discover that the kidney is the organ excretory of the urine, as Claudius Galen made it in the year 170; he can create a method of resolution of the quadratic equation, as al-Khowarizmi made it in 830; he can project a steamboat more than 550 years before Robert Fulton's steamship, as Roger Bacon made it around the year of 1250; he can have the role of leading a group of assistants who accompany him in the discovery of a great continent, as Christopher Columbus made it in 1492; he can invent and to market machines of adding, as Blaise Pascal made it in 1642; he can create a binary arithmetic which comes to be used two and a half centuries later in the architecture of the Von Neumann computers, as Leibniz made it in 1679; he can create the equations of speed and mass that will allow two and a half centuries later to maintain artificial stationary satellites rotating around the Earth to transmit signs of TV, cell-phone and internet, as Isaac Newton made it in 1686; it can fill a balloon of hot air and to fly over Lisbon, as Bartolomeu de Gusmao made it in his "passarola" in 1709; he can invent the vaccine, as Edward Anthony Jenner made it in 1796; he can decipher the cycle of the heat, allowing that half century later the refrigerator was created, as Sadi Carnot made it in 1824; he, in this case she, can try to help teacher Charles Babbage, manufacturer of calculators, inventing the programming language of computers, as August Ada Byron[1] made it in 1843; he can create an algebra to represent the whole Aristotelian Logic, as George Boole made it in 1847; he can discover how to represent the colors electronically, as James Clerk Maxwell made it 1855; he can recite "Mary had a little lamb" in front of a wax roll and to leave recorded this speech forever, as Thomas Alva Edison made it in 1877; he can produce in laboratory the electromagnetic waves discovered by Maxwell, as Heinrich Hertz made it in 1897; he can discover the capacity of transport of signs by the Hertzian waves, as Guglielmo Marconi made it in 1898; he can discover the way of translating in electric connections the connectives of the Boolean algebra, allowing that more ahead Alan Turing (1936), Konrad Zuse (1936), Claude Shannon (1937) and, finally, John Von Neumann (1946) represent the Logic in the computers, as Charles Sanders Peirce made it in 1902; he can point a bunch of light for the shovels of a small vane making it to rotate by receiving photons, then explaining the photoelectric effect, as Albert Einstein made it in 1905; he, in this case she, can discover the way of producing artificial radioactive elements, allowing to Otto Hahn four years later the discovery of the fission of the atom and to Enrico Fermi the creation of the first nuclear reactor (1942), as Irene Joliot-Curie made it in 1934; he, in this case she, can create a language of computation that uses words and human syntax, as Grace Murray Hopper made it in 1951; he can create the screen named liquid crystal display (LCD), as Pierre-Gilles made it in 1972; he can, with base in the Arpanet and the developing of the communication by electronic mail, create the Wide World Web (www) of the internet, as Timothy Berners-Lee made it in 1991; he can invent the artificial liver, as Kenneth Matsumura made it in 2001. All those things an individual, mobilizing his entire learning, he is able to do, alone or by leading a small group of people. But, unlike what economist Milton Friedman imagined during a lifetime, an alone man, even with a small team, doesn't provoke one long inflationary period simply printing money without ballast, because this theoretically irrefutable situation is not applied in practice. What creates chronic inflation is the city, the noxious capital, with all its new social class around the unhappy chief of State, who is seen, or by own will (Akhenaten), or by suffering imposition of an invader (Zhao Gou), or by inheriting the situation (Louis XVI), in distant area of the secular main capital of his land.

Reversion. When did the first registrations of the inflation of the paper money happen?

Even in the case of the voluntary transference of the chief of State for a noxious capital, he shouldn't be made responsible directly by the monetary tumult that the change provokes, because he wouldn't adopt such a capital if he had knowledge of the problem (knowledge is understood here not as a mere ownership of data, but as assimilated acceptance of concepts). In the case of Versailles, it is known that the revolutionaries brought Louis XVI on their shoulders, high dawn, to install him in the Palace of Louvre, in Paris. By the description of the scene, although historians try to give the idea that he was brought forcibly, the most appropriate reading is that the rescue of the traditional capital has been resolved in common agreement, as part of the revolutionary process, because the couple of monarchs' permanence in the Palace of Versailles came as an insult to the French. If Marie Antoinette liked her goats and her roses in the new-rich palace, this wasn't the case of Louis XVI, who tried not to contradict the revolutionaries' will, at least of the ones that didn't propose the end of the monarchy. And the escape of the Louvre, as everything indicates, was not idea of him, but of her (today it is known fact in the real estate industry that the decision on the place of couple's home is, in the almost totality of the cases, made by the wife). Concerning the case of the Song dynasty, the original capital, of the first period, was the city of Kaifeng. With the defeat for the Jin dynasty, the family Zhao had to be transferred and the new capital came to be Hangzhou, in the South. It was by this time, after 1127, more than one century after the adoption of the paper money, that the first registrations of the inflation appeared. One of the first ones studious, if not the first at all, to refer to the phenomenon was Ye Shi, who lived from 1150 to 1223. He accused the inflationary process of doing circulating an "empty currency" and of harming heavily the economy of the country.

Compromising. How did the inflation of Hangzhou commit the paper money?

As Ye Shi was born 23 years after the transfer of the capital, it can be deduced that the inflationary problem started to torment the life of Chinese of the South in a slow and gradual way. It is little probable also that Kaifeng, under the Jin dynasty, had abandoned a so practical use of the paper money and, if it didn't abandoned it, maintained the system without suffering any upset. The history played its light focus on the Southern Song that, with its emperor, the *huangdi*, installed in Hangzhou, the improvised capital, it had to live with a currency attacked by inflationary pulse. Another evident fact is that, if the Chinese money had presented great problems on this first century in Kaifeng, the new government organization in Hangzhou would have been insane if it had carried the invention for there. The automatic deduction is that the government would have returned to the metallism. The maintenance of the use of the paper money is the proof that in the first century it propitiated a great period of financial health. Losing the war for the Jin dynasty in 1127 means that this dynasty was stronger militarily, counting with support of the Northern Prefectures, not that the Song dynasty was worse financially. Under the new headquarters of the Empire, the subjects had to suffer per decades the insipidities brought by the pathologies of the currency of the noxious capital. In agreement with the estimates of Versailles-Weimar Effect's study, the problems can extend themselves for 120 years, or more, and, certainly, one century of suffering brought by a good invention surpasses a century previous of calm that his invention have propitiated.

Providences. Didn't the government make anything to stop the inflation?

Zhao Gou didn't attend in an impassive way to deterioration of the Chiao-Tzu. As well as the rulers make in the modern times, the currency was substituted by a new system. In 1161 one released the currency called Hui-Tzu (*check medium*), which was a paper money ballasted by reservation coinage, in copper. In little time the subjects were knowing there was not total correspondence among the values in circulation and the copper coins and, for losing not credibility, the government promised to control with iron fist the amount of paper money in circulation. During twenty years the system worked well and as result many other people in the world followed the rule. In Hangzhou, however, the inflationary pulse undermined this intelligent measure and the inflation returned, being this explained as a consequence of need of increases of military expenses, because nobody had knowledge of the Versailles-Weimar Effect. Under growing inflation, the Hui-Tzu fell in collapse in 1190. After the Mongolian invasion, which installed the Yuan dynasty, China only had more two dynasties, each with duration of approximately three centuries. Living together with the Song dynasty, in several parts of China, the Liao dynasty (916-1125) and the Jin dynasty (1115-1234) had place. And coming next the Song dynasty, China had the Yuan dynasty (1271-1368), the Ming dynasty (1368-1644) and the Qing dynasty (1644-1911), when then the Republic was proclaimed.

Capital. Were many the capitals of China in its history?

The dynasties matter for the study of the currency, but we have to analyze, with very larger attention, the changes of capitals for the emperors that were succeeded in those dynastic families. Until the beginning of the 20th century an average expression among Chinese gave account of having there been Four Great Old Capitals of China, and they were: Beijing, Nanjing, Luoyang and Chang'an. Among the years 1920 and 1930 other old capitals became considered and the expression came to be Seven Old Capitals of China, adding Kaifeng, Hangzhou and Anyang. These are capitals of great meaning in the Chinese history, but, among the several empires and in the several last times, Chinese had several dozens of capitals. For the present study it imports to bring to the light the succession of the capitals after the invention of the paper money. In this way, we have: (1) for the Yuan dynasty, Xanadu or Shangdu (1264-1276), Dadu (1276-1368) and again Xanadu (1368-1369); (2) for the Ming dynasty, Nanjing (1368-1421), Beijing (1421-1644), Nanjing (1644-1645), Fuzhou (1645-1646) and Zhaoqing (1646-1662); (3) for the Qing dynasty, Shengjing (1636-1644) and Beijing (1644-1911). We see that the Ming dynasty installed the capital in Beijing and there it stayed for more than two centuries, up to 1644, when it was substituted by the Qing dynasty, which there stayed until the end of the monarchy in December 29, 1911. The date 1661, considered as this in which the paper money was in force again without presenting problems, it could have happened, therefore, until one century before, because Beijing was already consolidated as capital. However, the republican government, initiated on January 1, 1912, maintained Beijing as capital only for thirteen years and, then, it befell a phase of several changes of presidential residences, culminating with the Chinese Revolution, in 1949. Without considering the moments in which two capitals were used at the same time, the list of the Chinese capitals after the end of the monarchy is the following: Beijing (1912), Guangzhou (1925), Wuhan (1927), Fengtian (1928), Nanjing (1928), Chongqing (1937), Nanjing (1946), Chongqing (1949), Chengdu (1949), Taipei (1949), Beijing (1949). With so many changes of capitals between 1925 and 1949, it is not difficult to see as the immense majority of the Chinese came to support the rebels of Mao Tse-Tung (or Mao Zedong) in his fight to take the power and to restore the residence of the chief of State in Beijing, what happened in 1949, leaving President Chiang Kai-shek with reduced number of followers and installed in Taipei, capital of the island of Formosa (Taiwan). Taipei represented the China in UN for 22 years, up to 1971, when it lost the seat for Beijing, that represents the continental China, or the Popular Republic of China.

2. The geocentric vision of the monetarism

Printing money produces the inflation; stopping printing doesn't eliminate it.

John Maynard Keynes: regulation for obtaining the full employment

Tentative. In the economy, the monetarism sought the middle term. Does this mean a success?

One cannot deny the merit of the monetarism by having looked for the middle way in several points of the economics. For instance, among choosing the neutrality of the currency, as the Austrian school of the business cycles wanted, and the political action, of the Keynesian Macroeconomics, Milton Friedman recognized the no-neutrality in the short period. However, this purpose of being seemingly in the middle didn't avoid that his approach was distanced of the correspondence with the heliocentric system: by the whole time, the vision was geocentric. How did this Ptolemaic system work? What was seen is what was described, nothing else. The Sun seemingly rotated around the Earth, therefore, Ptolemy guaranteed, the facts happened exactly like this. In the case of the monetarist inflation, the treatment was the same. The shortest of the humans agreed that if a ruler printed money in a systematic way, in volume always larger than the rate of necessary replacement to substitute damaged notes, and also larger than this allowed by the growth of the GDP, the result would be chronic inflation. This is what was seen and this is what was described, independently of any exogenous reasons. As the appearances deceive, just as in the geocentric system, the obvious prescription of the monetarism to solve the inflationary problem was to control the emission: no cent beyond what the GDP and the replacement allowed. The relativity of the referential systems, in the Mechanics of Galileo, led this scientist to rescue the heliocentric vision: it was not necessary landing in the surface of the Sun to see the movement of the planets around it, but just using imagination and deduction. The faith in the neutrality of the money in the long period was the board on which Friedman held for maintaining his geocentrism. For him, the neutral money in the long period could not be capable to engender any economical problem, what led him to deduce that the mistake was in the ruler's free will of issuing notes. If he could make the decision of emitting beyond the account, he would be able to, with the same freedom, to emit a volume on this side of the necessary. As in the geocentric system, the equations presented coherence. There was not internal mistake in the theory. The problem was: it didn't help to solve any problem that transcends the atmosphere of the perfection. The model was correct, but it could not be extended. Any vehicle that escaped from the terrestrial orbit would see the uselessness of the arrangement.

Practical. Why was not the monetarism a practical model in the combat to the inflation?

The prescription of Friedman didn't work for a very simple reason: the inflationary emission was not a decision dictated by a problem of bad character or of the ruler's ignorance. If it would be like this, it would be enough to change the agent by somebody of good temper. When, finally, in the years 1990, rulers of countries inflamed by hyperinflation achieved to outline the problem, by using heterodox methods, and no more the orthodox methods of the monetarism, by prudence and by respect to the work of Friedman they were very careful on the subject of the money emission. The meaning of this is that the theory of Friedman didn't give instruments to abolish the inflation, but, once the inflationary pulse was tamed, the recommendation of the control of the emission was something one could not ignore. The sympathetic Nobel Prize's bearer gave, therefore, his contribution to the conquest of the monetary stabilization, but not in the way like he would like to have seen, without the contribution of the heterodoxy in the crucial moment of the supposed cure of the terrible disease. It is important to have in account that the problem resolved in this phase was that of taming, not the one of eliminating, the inflationary pulse. So much is like this that the countries which escaped from the hyperinflation stayed in permanent fight against the ghost of the turn of the increase of the inflation rates, with high expenses and skilled financial mechanisms being used without truce. The disconnection of which Keynes accused the classic economics in relation to the practical world was present in the monetarist economics, because Friedman rejected of Keynes exactly the aspect related to the political intervention on the money, once he believed in its neutrality in the long period. By this belief, he was impeded of noticing something stunningly visible, which was the fact that, if the ruler printed money without ballast by some interest, he, ruler, no matter how imbecile was, he knew that he was taking the worst of the roads in the practice of the deviations of conduct. The called "power of the pen", the possibility of the influence traffic and the officialization of illicit earnings - as Elizabeth I made in relation to the pillagers of the seas -, these are some of the unscrupulous ruler's many manners to abuse of their position and to increase their richness immeasurably, without provoking the popular anger, what is the more immediate political return in front of the appearance of an inflationary period.

Perceptions. Doesn't the history give Friedman reason?

For Friedman, the inflationary climbing was a conscious choice on the part of the ruler, one stupid choose, that he was able very well to disentangle himself. It was not this, certainly, the perception of Zhao Gou, forced to create a new court in Hangzhou, once expelled from his old and good Kaifeng. It wasn't this the perception of Romulus Augustulus, heir of a fragile throne in the noxious capital Ravenna, when he took knowledge of the invasion of Rome in 476 by the barbarians. As well as it was not this the perception of Louis XVI, who inherited the fatidic Versailles of his father and his grandfather, when changing his minister of finances times without account, having Turgot among them, and when seeing the discharge of prices more and more out of control, until the revolt that led to the Storming of the Bastille in 1789 and, three years later, to his beheading. And after so many tragic histories, would Friedrich Ebert agree in printing notes in the Republic of Weimar in volume that provoked until that moment the larger inflationary climbing in the human history? Because the people when carrying to the market the pushcart to do purchases didn't carry it empty, but loaded of notes. Friedman, certainly, could use the example of his own country, that established the gold standard when it faced the possibility of exaggerating emissions and, in a certain way, it managed to do the North American citizens' life to be not so disrupted, but he should also have observed that the inflation in the United States even so was not put down, until it came the measure of the control of prices of the Keynesian John Kenneth Galbraith, in 1942, what led to the full employment of 1944. Obviously, Friedman preferred the gold standard (instituted in 1792 by Alexander Hamilton and abolished officially in 1971) to the politics of Galbraith, but he knew that the Hui-Tzu, having the copper as standard, was also ruined in the 12th century. And, after all, the North American rulers were so humans as the Chinese ones were, with all their weaknesses and their cares.

Periods. At what do differ the conceptions of short period in Keynes and in Friedman?

Friedman, with his search of the middle term, was criticized so much by the conservatives as by the progressives, more for these than for those. The first ones, followers of the Austrian school of the business cycles, didn't understand like Friedman could support fiscal and monetary politics, reconciling this with his positions of man averse to the government's interference in the markets. The second ones saw how negative point of his macroeconomic theory the fact of being used to give sustaining to brutal regimes, as the military dictatorship of Chile, initiated in 1973. He could not admit this, but in those authoritarian regimes his recommendations not worked by they have some contact point with the practical world, but by they be implemented under hard repression. The argument of exemption of him was the fact that, at least, those dictatorships were not leftist, but he should have noticed that there was something of very wrong with his model, which was combined so well with dictatorial regimes. He justified it saying that he rejected of the Keynesianism "only" the part regarding the political intervention, because, he said, the economists should not give action's instructions to the rulers, but simply to wait that the voters, with all their power of decision, chose those whose proposals more seemed correct and fair to them. In that point he acted as that individual who says himself "impolitic" and allows making preaching on this, trying to win followers for his cause, which is "political". His monetarist theory, that absorbed of the Keynesianism the action's proposal in the short period, renounced the fact that the true middle term was the Keynesian macroeconomics, which came, in an explicit way, as the alternative to the dilemma of the years 1920, between the conservative liberals' classic economy and the revolutionaries' planned economy. Short period for Friedman was the horizon of action because, according to him, only in this phase the money is not neutral. According his allegory of the helicopter, one aircraft of that type that spills coins in an island will improve the inhabitants' income in the first month of the feat, but, in the following months, repeating the experience, it will just create inflation, because the commerce will increase prices. The idea of short period in Keynes referred itself to the fact that this was the limit on which the economy could make prognostics, once government and market cannot escape from the darkness of the uncertainty, although they can lessen it. The institutions, sustained by the contracts, can give warranties of operation of the economy in the short period, but the almost totality of the contracts has alone validity in this period. For instance, workers can be relieved in the beginning of a crisis when the company that employs them has substantial orders to be accomplished inside of the fiscal exercise in subject. But they know that, if the crisis lasts long, new contracts will stop being signed between the company and their customers, and this will mean the end of their labor agreements. In this way, although the uncertainty is the same next minute and next decade, the institutions accomplish their obligations for some months, but, in general, they don't have as sustaining commitments of long period. This was theme of the "mathematical" part of the Keynesianism, which Friedman said not to have how objecting. The disagreement in the "political" part was in the following: Keynes developed all his theory as an instrumental one that allowed to the government and the civil society to reduce to the maximum, for the largest possible period, the circumstance of the countries be submitted to the unpleasant surprises come of the uncertainty, always in agreement with Bertrand Russell's teaching, according to who institutions as school, planning family and other human inventions are defense mechanisms against the cruelty of the natural selection. Adopting, therefore, the Keynes' mathematical tools and to reject his political-philosophical position is equal to be worth of the temperate scale of Johann Sebastian Bach, being thankful to him for this, but despising their compositions.

Power. Many accused Keynes by the hyperinflations of the years 1960-1980. Were they right?

Under the belief of the classic economics in relation to the neutrality of the money, belief maintained by the Austrian school and by the neoclassicist followers of Walras and Pareto, and still under the validity of the Say's Law (everything that will be produced will be bought), which was extended until the Great Depression of 1929, the instruction that the governments received was that they didn't have control on the operation of the money, although they learned on the role of the liquidity and the interest rates, always in inverted vision concerning to the true meaning of those facts. To solve a great problem of retraction of the economy, the prescription that they had was the one of reducing the public works, restricting the liquidity and increasing the interests, in a way to remove the government of the transactions among the market's agents. In situation of labor's unemployment and idle capacity of the factories, this formula was equal to supply poison to the dying ones. It was like this in the crisis of 1929, as Friedman himself recognized it. Keynes knew, after the publication of the "General Theory of Employment, Interests and Money", in 1936, that, if the book was recognized and cultivated, the world would not see more any other economical crisis in the proportions of the Great Depression of 1929, because the empire of the uncertainty no longer would be cultivated in fertile land, given that the "General Theory" showed the road to transform the use of the money in combat's instrument against the economical retractions. He taught the governments how to use the power on the currency to put down the crises. They who thought the money was neutral and imperturbable, they learned that it is instrument of political action. Now, accusing Keynes for the hyperinflations in the second half of the 20th century is the same as to blame Becquerel, Rutherford, Marie Curie, Irene Joliot-Curie and Enrico Fermi for the dead of Hiroshima and Nagasaki under the atomic bomb. Keynes, who saw the inflation as one of the most serious problems of social corrosion, he only showed that the government should use its power on the currency. If some government was worth of this teaching to blame Keynes for the inflation rate, this just made choir to the preaching of Friedman, who saw as origin of the exaggerating and continuous emission of money the mere character of laxity moral of the ruler. Of course the economy suffers interferences of the morals, free will, care and idiosyncrasies of individual agents, when those agents are holders of the power, but those factors are diluted before larger imperatives of causes and effects, which belong to the domain of Physics, Biology, Ethology and Social Psychology.

Coherence. Was there mistake in the conceptions cultivated by the economists about the inflation?

The studies about inflation from the years 1930 to 1990 brought deep and necessary knowledge on the theme and, in general, sustained in good use of mathematical instruments, they presented internal coherence and they had their mistakes corrected in this same period. This was the case of the Phillips Curve, which correlated, by statistical studies, falls in the inflation rates with falls in the job rates. Friedman showed the flaws of the model and he gave his corrected version, in the curve named of "augmented expectations", confronting, like he himself explains, the conclusions of the Phillips Curve with the attendance of the Brazilian inflationary process of the years 1960. Before this, in 1956, Phillip Cagan's Hypothesis was already revealed empirically solid: he related the intensity of the inflation rate to the expectation in the market of the rate of replacement of the money. Those conclusions, allied to writings of Keynes, Galbraith, Robert Solow, Edmund Phelps and other, allowed Mário Henrique Simonsen to formulate the theory of the inertial inflation and, in consequence, to help young Brazilian economists to develop effective strategies in the confrontation of the problem. Finally, mistakes in the formulations were moved away. It was not this the question. The entire problem was in the fact that the production of the inflation was not something so mechanic as Milton Friedman's preaching led to understand. It was necessary to see the situation of the point of view of the heliocentrism.

3. The Brazilization of South America

The social inequality of Brasilia was spread for the neighboring countries.

Mario Henrique Simonsen: concept of the inertial inflation

Disparity. What primordial factor did provoke the immense inequality that is seen in Brazil?

In the year 1960, a Brazilian ruler, named Kubitschek, elected in agreement with the pathology of the Republics of Tutelage, i. e., by the majority direct popular vote, which destroys the federation idea, he inaugurated the new capital of Brazil in the central area of the country, abandoning the capital that few years before reached the secular majority, Rio de Janeiro. The inflationary climbing didn't expect the inauguration of the city. Since the beginning of the construction of Brasilia, two years before, with the President's frequent permanences in the construction site, it was clear for the population that the center of the power was moved. In the beginning, what one had was the heavy costliness. Popular complaints and constant claims of the unions pressed the government to take some providence. Lowering the prices? It is enough to read the "General Theory" to know that there is not this possibility. It would be the correct measure if we always thought in agreement with the geocentric model. Keynes, however, affirms that the workers' demand in general is for larger wages, not for smaller prices (certainly a first by-product of the "monetary illusion", identified by Irving Fisher in the United States). In those circumstances, the president called to his palace the supporting leader Ulysses Guimaraes to inform that he didn't see other way except ordering to print money. It was begun in this moment the race that transformed costliness in inflation and this in hyperinflation, in a process that afflicted Brazilians for almost four decades. Along the path the socioeconomic differences increased in a brutal way, what led André Gorz to create the term "Brazilization", to express that disparity. In the 21st century, something similar begins to happen with Nigeria, by its new capital Abuja, since 1991; with Myanmar, through its recent capital Naypyidaw, since 2005; and with Zimbabwe and its new presidential palace in Borrowdale Brook, since 2006. Brussels won't lead to a very different situation in Europe, beginning by the accentuation of the difference of economical level among States more developed and States of the South, starting with the most southern among the continental ones, that is Greece.

Illusion. Why didn't the money impression solve the problem of the costliness?

In the mind of the salary earners, the monetary illusion leads to the belief that is better to struggle for receiving more remuneration, when the prices increase, than to demand a fall in the prices. Inside the inflationary process, the other groundless belief is that when receiving incomes of interests added of readjustments by the inflation, there were more earnings than the mere interest rate. But don't only the workers and the popular investors suffer of monetary illusion. The rulers also let deceive themselves. Like this it was that the Brazilian government gave beginning to the inflationary climbing. With base in the conservative liberals of the Austrian school of the business cycles (Friedman was little known at that time), this government believed animatedly in the solution of the impression ad hoc. It didn't pass by the rulers' mind that such a measure was equal to kill Nosferatu, when the death of the body just means the transfer of the spirit for another human body, maintaining itself the saga of the vampire, although with new appearance. The money impression, done in the exterior, didn't solve the problem because the phenomenon observed on those days was not an accidental costliness, but a psychological process, which is today known as inflationary pulse. Even if there is not any perspective of money impression, the costliness continue growing until the limit of the bearable, leading to a terrible situation of social poverty. The role of the money replacement since then was that of serving as solace in the relentless process of Brazilization. It was as spilling of times in times water of some truck-pipe in the fire, so that it didn't exterminate the forest very quickly. From 1930 to 1994 the Brazilian inflation rate reached the accumulated figure of 100 quadrillion percent (the number one followed by seventeen zeros), leading several times to the cut of three zeros in the face value of the money. The inflation, at last, is not an independent monetary disease: it is the fever.

Recrudescence. What events did have room in the first years of the inflation of Brasilia?

Brazilians didn't walk during those inflationary decades in a lineal road. Many mechanisms were created with views to the extermination of the disease, but almost all of them just mitigated the pains, reducing the fever. In the end of the year 1960, lawyer Janio Quadros, admirer, at the same time, of Mussolini and Che Guevara, was chosen President. He took office in the beginning of 1961 and just governed by one semester, resigning on August 25, being substituted temporarily by the President of the Chamber of Deputies Paschoal Ranieri Mazzilli. His vice president, Joao Goulart, elected together with him, but in independent way, and also by the majority direct vote, was in China in the day of the title-holder's renouncement and came to take office on September 7, on the condition that he would adopt the parliamentary system, that should be confirmed later in popular consultation. The solution of the parliamentarism was negotiated by the chief of the Military House of the interim presidency, general Ernesto Geisel, between the political leaders and the military commanders, since these had promised to impede the vice president installation at all costs. Four prime ministers later (Tancredo Neves, Brochado da Rocha, Moura Andrade and Hermes Lima – Moura Andrade just during 24 hours), the foreseen plebiscite took place in January 1963, revoking the parliamentarism, when then Joao Goulart started to accumulate the leaderships of government and State. Governing under the presidentialism, Goulart proposed in February 1964 a nominal increase of 100% on the minimum wage, measure that repeated one that he had taken ten years before when he occupied the position of Minister of Work of the Getulio Vargas' government, and whose consequences led the chief to resign. This time the result was the worsening of the inflation rate, because now the court of supporting of the presidency of the Republic was the upstarts' class of the new capital. In the dawn of April 1, 1964, under several subterfuges, the Brazilian National Congress decreed the vacancy of the president position, seating on the presidential chair the president of the Chamber of Deputies, Ranieri Mazzilli. The accusations against Joao Goulart included illegalities, break of military hierarchy, attempt of hitting the Constitution to do land reform and authority lack. The true motivating factor for the coup d'état of April 1 was the inflation, which certainly would lead to a new blow if Deputy Ranieri Mazzilli was maintained in the presidency. On April 10, the press still greeted as "Hero of the Revolution" the governor of the State of Minas Gerais, banker Magalhaes Pinto, but neither this governor nor the president-in-office had prestige and authority for sustaining the new political configuration under situation of inflationary climbing. Therefore, the military of higher patent were convinced to endorse the coup d'état, once they had helped to sustain Joao Goulart's deposition, supporting the governors of Minas Gerais, Guanabara (the city of Rio de Janeiro, that then was a State of the federation) and State of Sao Paulo and, more than this, they had resisted to the threat of using the force to close the National Congress done by the Minister of the Civil House Darcy Ribeiro in the dawn of April 1 in the case of the parliamentarians to decreed the president's deposition. In this way, in the day April 11 the National Congress chose to the presidency of the Republic marshal Humberto de Alencar Castello Branco, with inauguration on April 15, giving start to the military regime, which would last 21 years and would have in its direction five officials of the Army as chiefs of State.

Measures. What initial steps did the military ones take against the inflation?

The first military president of the regime of 1964 had intention of "putting the house in order" and soon accomplishing normal elections and returning the power to the civilians in the time determined by the Constitution, completing the term initiate then by Janio Quadros and continued by Joao Goulart and Ranieri Mazzilli. This was not the thinking of other military commanders, there being among them the ones that glimmered a minimum period of twenty years for the "sanitation" of the sore spots of the country. They intended to cure the national life of the evils of:

(A) corruption,
(B) demagogy,
(C) inflation,
(D) underdevelopment,
(E) illiteracy.

They also chose as opponent the group of the forces that struggled for the implantation of the socialism. In this way, the military ones created a doctrine for their mission: (a) they settled as date of the coup d'état March 31, alleging to have there been a displacement of troops from the city of Juiz de Fora, in Minas Gerais, towards the State of Rio de Janeiro (in any other phase, this would be a routine displacement); (b) they created the expression "redeemer revolution", to substitute the coup d'état idea; (c) they convinced the historians that their intervention in the leadership of the State began in this date from March 31, not on April 11; (d) they preached their objective of implementing their fixing politics; (e) finally, they were convinced of the no-contradiction between their purpose of struggling for the legality and the acceptance of a presidency resulting from coup d'état, once they were just solving a problem of vacuum of power. If that was not written with all of the letters in the official documents, it is like this that the facts happened. Castello Branco governed the country until March 15, 1967, and, among the measures against the inflation, taken by the Ministers Roberto Campos, of Planning, and Octavio Gouveia de Bulhoes, of Finance, were: reduction of public expenses, incentive to the exports, attraction of external investments, collection increase, repeal of the Law of Remittance of Profits and extinction of the employment stability (the stability, of the era of the Getulism, that was gotten after ten years in the same job, was substituted by the Fund of Warranty by Time of Service). This orthodox prescription got to promote a substantial reduction of the inflation rates. The two ministers, although they had made acquaintance with Keynes in the Bretton Woods Conference, in 1944, stayed linked to an economical line practiced by conservative liberals.

Cut. When did happen the first money change in the Brazilian military regime?

The inflation rates were lowered, but they continued tormenting the Brazilians. In this way, on February 13, still in the government Castello Branco, one month before the following government's office, of marshal Costa e Silva, it was proceeded to a cut of three zeros in the currency, which had changed the name of Cruzeiro (Big Cross) for New Cruzeiro and it passed to be printed in Rio de Janeiro. The notes in circulation were not substituted, but just stamped with the new name and the new face value. In the day of the presidential inauguration, March 15, the name of the country was also changed, from Republic of the United States of Brazil to Federative Republic of Brazil. The new currency won relative stability, but the repression passed to do itself present more and more in the two following years, until on December 13, 1968, the Number Five Institutional Act (AI-5) was signed, giving to the president the power to take any decision, without owing obedience to the Constitution or any other law. This was the establishment of the dictatorship, which only came officially to be weakened on January 1, 1979, with the repeal of that instrument. On that year, 1968, the inflation was lowered for 22.0%, against 91.8% in 1964. On August 31, 1969, President Costa e Silva fell sick and a committee of three generals started to command the country, until the oath of office of the following president, general Emilio Garrastazu Medici, on October 30. The five years of the term of Medici were characterized by the increasing hardening of the regime. Under the empire of the fear, the economy experienced a period of good growth, period that was called of "Brazilian Miracle". In 1970 the currency returned to the name Cruzeiro, without loss of zeros, and, in the final of 1973, the inflation, that continued to decrease, presented annual rate of 15.7% (or 13.0%, in the index of the Getulio Vargas Foundation), as a result of subsidy to the wheat (1972) and combined orthodox politics with repressive political regime. This panorama inspired the military coup d'état of Chile, on September 11, 1973, and the military coup d'état of Argentina, this on March 24, 1976.

Subsidy. Was the inflation under control in the following government?

After the oath of office of the general Ernesto Geisel in the presidency of the Republic in March 15, 1974, the inflation presented a slow growth in its rates again. The guerrilla of Araguaia had been put down in the end of the Médici's government and now President Geisel promised a distention of the regime, in a politics that, months later, would be called "slow, gradual and safe opening". A minor repression was accompanied by a larger increasing of prices. However, the Minister of Finance, Mario Henrique Simonsen, enlarged the subsidy to the wheat consumption in 1977, obtaining with this a reduction in the rhythm of the inflation growth. The rate was not more in the proximity of the one that was registered in 1973, which was a number in the range of the critical level, number above which the prices are pushed upward and below which they are pulled down, but it was an inflationary growth that didn't bring great irritations to the population, because the housewives could see the prices of the rice maintaining itself unaffected during weeks, and the price of the bread, with subsidized wheat, resisting without increases by several months. What came in the following government, however, was something that the Brazilian people could not longer forget. One of President Geisel's favorite ministers was the general Reynaldo Melo de Almeida, writer Jose Americo de Almeida's son, old friend of the president. Everything implied that the general Almeida would be indicated by Geisel to be the successor, but in certain moment he made a critic that displeased Geisel. It was necessary to look for another name, and then Geisel gave in to the appeals of the barracks and indicated general Joao Figueiredo, a general Euclydes Figueiredo's son. Geisel had abolished the AI-5 and announced the political opening, besides having governed with an opposition majority, because, in the first election to the Parliament of his period, the "Brazilian Miracle" had already been dissipated and the country faced the first petroleum crisis, situation that led the president to create the Program of the Combustible Alcohol more ahead. The opposition got then to do most of the seats, for the first time since the beginning of the military regime. Society hoped the president put an end to the military governments' sequence and announced a civil candidate to his succession. But, before even of announcing the name of general Figueiredo, he had said: It is still necessary that the successor is a military man.

Amnesty. Did the successor in the presidency maintain or contradict Geisel's politics?

The presidential term, which was quinquennial until Geisel's mandate, it came to be settled in six years for the successor. Joao Figueiredo took office on March 15, 1979, and soon he showed his differences in relation to President Geisel, so much that in certain time he let off steam: This boy is making everything to the opposite. One of the disagreement points in the politics of the new agent was the treatment to the convicts of the dictatorship. Geisel, with the opening, had begun the process of revision of penalties, what made many political prisoners to leave the jails and many exiled to return to the country, this being the case of the former-minister Darcy Ribeiro, the gaucho former-governor Leonel Brizola and the former-president of the National Union of Students Jose Serra. Instead to maintain and to enlarge the politics of the revisions, Figueiredo allied to the liberals that were asking for the wide, general and unrestricted amnesty. The position difference between revision and amnesty was that the regime, by the first option, recognized that it had been in mistake and it was correcting its path, while the second option reaffirmed the success of the regime in condemning its contestant ones and now it forgave them, generously, through the requested amnesty. This second vision was the one that prevailed, leading the Parliament to approve the amnesty law, which granted the benefit to the two sides of the fight, and made them, three decades later, Brazilians, envying the punishments that Argentinians and Chileans ministered to their former dictators, to lament and try to review that law, which was so well received in that time. The other disagreement point referred to the Republic of Tutelage. Geisel several times affirmed that the country still had not experimented the democratic regime, and that this should be built. Figueiredo and other liberals thought, to the opposite, that the Republic of Tutelage (or Cassock), lived between 1946 and 1961, was an oasis that should be revisited at all the cost. He was openly favorable to the turn of the majority direct election to the presidency, but he knew that he didn't have enough prestige to approve the measure during his mandate. He didn't get tired, however, of promising the turn of that 'paradise', as soon as the conditions allowed, and, among the adverse conditions, were Geisel, the pro-regime parliamentarians and the Superior School of War (ESG). The reading of this presidential vision encouraged the masses, which started to promote great mass assemblies in favor of the approval of the "Direct Now!", while guided by oppositionist politicians and by soccer's players and soccer's speakers. All of the demonstrators were nostalgic of that electoral game of the Republics of Tutelage. The amendment was voted in the end of Figueiredo's mandate and it was rejected by the Parliament, but only for a matter of moment. It had been very clear that the next voting, after a new submission of the matter, would guarantee the majority direct election for the successor's successor.

Resurgence. How was the inflation rate during Joao Figueiredo's term?

The complete aversion to the experiments on the part of President Figueiredo led him to revisit methods, politics, auxiliary ones and past eras. Ministers who were long time ago far away from the administration were called to Brasilia and again they were vested as title-holders of offices. The petroleum crisis had weakened the international economy and the little administration capacity caught Brazil unprotected. The Minister Mario Henrique Simonsen's dismissal completed the board of abandonment in which the national economy was thrown, and the country watched impotent to the resurgence of the process of inflationary acceleration. As answer to the crisis and also as coherence point with the liberal politics, the subsidy to the wheat was removed little by little, between 1980 and 1982. It was the last military term inside the plan of two decades of intervention forged in the ESG. The generals could return the power to the civilians in a self-reliant way, presenting a "sanitated" country, as they glimpsed in 1964, or they could make this in an embarrassed way, certain that they failed in their task. Yes, in the first fifteen years of military regime the country had left the condition of exporter of agricultural products exclusively for the one of exporter of industrialized goods. But now, in 1982, the retraction period began what was known later as "the lost decade". Of the rate of 40.84% registered in 1978, at the end of the Geisel's government, the annual inflation reached in the end of 1983 the rate of 211%. High inflation, recession and debt crisis composed the economical board of the decline of the Figueiredo's government. For larger anguish of the chief of State, the president of the pro-regime party, Senator Jose Sarney, writer and former-governor of the State of Maranhao, was conquered by the opponents, after many audiences with Deputy Ulysses Guimaraes, president of the opposition party, and came to compose the platform of the candidate to the presidency, Tancredo Neves, in the position of candidate to vice presidency. With Tancredo Neves victorious in the election accomplished in the National Congress and impeded of taking office due to a serious illness, the political forces of the Parliament, in agreement with the Minister of the Army, General Leonidas Pires Goncalves, decided to give office to the chosen vice-president Jose Sarney in the day foreseen for the transmission of positions, that was March 15, 1985. Figueiredo, by respect to the ceremonial, would have to pass the presidential strip to Jose Sarney. By shame, displeasure or obstinacy of bad loser, Figueiredo refused to give the strip, which Sarney came to receive of other hands.

Plane. Did the civil government take some more serious providence against the inflation?

The inauguration of Sarney, as vice-president, sought to assure, before everything, the transition for the civil regime. Many in the government defended the postponement of the office, for when Tancredo received discharge of the hospital, but the prudence led to the finishing of the regime in the expected date. Tancredo stayed interned and died on April 21, so that Sarney became President since then. His period, in agreement with the rules of the presidential election of those days, would be of six years, but he proposed reduction for four years. Years later he struggled arduously to enlarge for five years, and he got the approval of that demand in the Parliament, but it would have been much better for him to pass the office after a quadrennial period. Because the plan of economical stabilization implemented by him in the second year of the mandate, the Cruzado Plan, of February 28, 1986, it had short life and the measures that came later presented insignificant results in comparison with the earnings of 1986. The Cruzado Plan consisted of the change of the currency Cruzeiro (big cross) for the Cruzado (crusader), with cut of three zeros in the face value, accompanied of freezing of prices, without date to finish. Inspired in models already applied in Israel and Argentina, and formulated by economists Joao Sayad, Francisco Lopes, Persio Arida and Andre Lara Resende, having then as guarantor and public relations the Minister of Finance, industrial entrepreneur Dilson Funaro, the plan soon recruited wide support of the population, tired of seeing always its wage disappear before the end of the month, consumed by the inflation. Therefore they appeared rumors that the prices freeze would be revoked in the month of May, but Funaro noticed that he needed to deny this information, because to settle a close date for the liberation of the prices would mean to invite industrial and merchants to establish the night of changing prices and the inflation would again return with redoubled force. The citizens went shopping with the table of prices in their hands, and they denounced the abuses that by chance they found. The most determined in that task composed the big group that came to be called "Sarney's controllers", controllers that dispersed themselves by the whole country. On that year 1986 the industry passed by a dizzy growth, and the number of open firms in a same year was the largest registered already in the Brazilian history.

Risks. Was the inflationary pulse tamed with that new currency?

In the month of July, Joao Sayad, Who was Minister of Planning, made a risky decision, that could commit the prices freeze if it would be badly interpreted by the consumer: he instituted a compulsory loan of 28% on the price of the fuels. The trust that the population deposited in the drivers of the plan led it to interpret that increment as a tribute, not as one price increase, and the Cruzado continued unharmed. With base in the success of that experience, in November Funaro announced increase of taxes on alcoholic drinks and tobacco. That could have been accept of the same form that the tribute on the fuels, but to that time a phenomenon permeated of bad citizenship already corroded the new currency: powerful merchants were well supervised and denounced when they disobeyed to the pricing tables, but the small merchants, as the owners of kiosks, bars, snack bars and small restaurants, these were unknown in their transgressions. In December it had already been clear for everyone that the freezing no more would be sustained. It was like this that the beginning of the year 1987 found the country in its insane work of thawing the prices that were stable in 1986 and the turn of the macroeconomic difficulties led Minister Funaro to declare moratorium of one year in the service of the foreign debt. The freezing was not effective in the task of taming the inflationary pulse, but the learning that the government and the economists had on that year was valuable in the following attempts of building combat mechanisms to the chronic inflation.

Apprenticeship. Did the government Sarney's economists take good advantage of that experience?

That learning would come to have good use in the following years, but not in the Sarney government. In 1987 Minister Dilson Funaro died of cancer and then other ministers of Finance came. On that same year, already without Funaro, the government released a system of readjustments called Unit of Reference of Prices (URP), according to which the prices would be readjusted quarterly, at most, by the geometric average of the inflation of the three precedent months. That was just an attempt of riding the dragon, as one called the inflationary pulse, without being burned by the fires of its mouth, but that didn't present result that one could appreciate. In 1989, new plan was presented. As Argentina had released the Spring Plan, Brazil released the Summer Plan, changing the Cruzado for the New Cruzado, with new cut of three zeros in the face value. With a prices freeze that was neither respected by the merchants nor supervised by the consumers, this plan in nothing helped, except in the facilitation of the use of the calculators for sake of the reduction of three digits, once the accounts in the previous currency difficultly fitted in the viewer. The annual inflation of 1989 was 1782.8%.

Bills. Would not the solution be to restrict the liquidity drastically in the market?

First elected President by majority direct vote since 1960, economist Fernando Collor de Mello took office in March 15, 1990, promising to end the inflation dragon with a single shot and, as he only had a bullet in the needle, he informed that could not wander. With an eminently orthodox prescription, but, just in case, incorporating the heterodox idea of prices freeze, the Collor Plan I seemed at the beginning to bring the solution for the old problem of the hyperinflation. By the kidnapping during eighteen months, called improperly to the time a confiscation, of all of the bank deposits, of natural or juridical persons, which exceeded the equivalent to little more than 50 dollars, the plan sought to disable the growth of the inflation rate through a brutal restriction of the liquidity. In that Plan, the money lost three zeros once again, it stopped being called New Cruzado and returned to be Cruzeiro. In the first weeks the trade took the appearance of ghost city, with empty stores and commercial streets finally deserted. Without access to the bank accounts, merchants and consumers rediscovered the simple change. Entrepreneurs paid wages with goods, real estate changed houses for apartments and the credit to the consumer solved the problem of the liquidity lack. If the Collor Plan I had worked, the President would have been greeted as the man who abolished the inflation and, at the same time, the job. It is not possible to know if he would come to be admired by that fact. As it didn't work, most of the voters started to hate him. Under the resurgence of the pulse of the inflationary climbing, the Minister of the Economy, Zelia Cardoso de Mello, released the Collor Plan II, or Zelia Plan, a new freezing of prices, without currency change, but just with the objective of playing government's actions without new unpleasant surprises for the economical agents. She became prime minister de facto, although the government was not parliamentary. Because of a courtship in a certain dance in Brasilia, the Minister discharged, and nobody else could save the President's term. Gathered with more than a hundred chiefs of State in Rio de Janeiro, where he returned the federal capital to during fifteen days, in the Conference Echo-92, or Rio-92, in the month of July, the President could not foresee what was drawn in his political horizon. Of turn to the noxious capital, he accompanied, of his cabinet in the Plateau Palace, in September 1992, the approval by the Parliament of the presidential impediment, for sake of administrative improbity, and vice-president Itamar Franco was vested as new President.

Proof. If emitting money does produce inflation, stopping printing doesn't solve the problem?

If Milton Friedman paid attention to the Collor Plan I, he must have been convinced, although didn't admitted it, that the rigid controls of the liquidity and the money impression don't serve as weapon against the chronic inflation in the era of the special check and the credit card.

As already explained in the book "Ten ways to abolish the inflation" (1993), it deals about a logical error of application of the notion of double implication, although Friedman was bachelor in Mathematics: exaggerating impression of money to produce inflation doesn't implicate, as he imagined, that the impression absence necessarily eliminates the inflation rate. In this case, as it is said in the mathematical circles, it is not worth the reverse. As well as the overproduction without buyer in the crisis of 1929 dropped the Say's Law, the ineffectiveness of Collor's measure in the combat to the inflation undressed the fallacy of the "Friedman's prescription". Economist Friedman could argue that the prices freeze were a strange element to his recommendations, but Collor, when increasing this item, was right, by the experience of the last plans, that pure orthodox prescription would be pure waste of time in situation of obstinate hyperinflation. After all, they were thirty years of fruitless attempts.

Criticality. Could not the liquidity lack have created the habit of maintaining stable the prices?

Even if the plan had gotten to reduce the inflation rate for a number below the critical index, there would be other factors to control, and what they would be it were not still clear in the moment. The economists that recognize the existence of the critical index don't have a magic number to show to represent this value, but they know that it is something among annual 10% and 13%, what gives a monthly index in the range that is going from .95% to 1.00%. If the inflation exceeds 1% in each month during following months (annual 12.68%), or it oscillates around a value above this average, maintaining stable the prices will cart great losses for the entrepreneurs, it is why that value pulls the inflation rate upward. If, to the opposite, the index of increase of prices maintains itself for the following months below the monthly average of 1%, the increases of prices can drive away the customers, which will seek stores that have maintained stable their prices, bringing losses for the merchant that increases prices, and this pulls the inflation rate down. With rate above the critical index, the consumers don't have alternative, and they are forced to buy products with renewed prices always. In the contrary situation, the good news run, and they will make their purchases in the stores that offer lower prices, as it happened in 1986 during the validity of the Cruzado Plan.

Siege. Could the successive and varied plans lead to a more functional anti-inflation siege?

As well as the copper standard allowed Hangzhou to control the Hui-Tzu for twenty years and as well as the gold standard gave some relief to the United States along the 120 initial years of its capital Washington, since it was rebuilt in 1812, after the fire that English submitted it (the North American population didn't take it a lot in account since its installation, in 1800, and the fire did that it came to be defended), the several attack plans struck against the inflation in the 20th century would have to produce effect in some moment. Along the year 1993 the inflation continued growing, but President Itamar Franco, an engineer that had already been governor of Minas Gerais, had the firm purpose of putting the economy in the railways and, so, this year was used so that the economists, of the government and of the market, intensified the debate on which path should be followed. In the first months of the new government, the president moved of the Ministry of the Foreign Relations to the Ministry of Finance sociologist Fernando Henrique Cardoso, not because of his knowledge of Economics, which was not a lot, but by his recognition in the intellectual world and by his leadership capacity. When questioned on his domain in the macroeconomic area, the new Minister of Finance alleged he was professor of History of the Economical Thought, in the College of Economy and Administration of the University of Sao Paulo (FEA-USP), and for sake of this he was not like this so lay in the matter. Far away from forming in the ministry a team of stars of the academy, Cardoso allocated in key posts professors of important research centers, but people without arrogance, capable to read and to respect the proposals that circulated in the cabinets on those days, with that humility that Keynes complained of his critics. It is very possible that those technicians have been chosen like this so that they didn't make shadow on him, but Fernando Henrique Cardoso got right in full with this attitude, because this characteristic was fundamental in the patient and very articulate making of what would be the Real Plan. Still in 1993 the name of the currency was changed of Cruzeiro for Real Cruzeiro, without the population to have account that was just part of a transition. In October the universal indexer was released, with the name of Real Unit of Value (URV). It was the Abstract Unit presented in the book "Ten ways to abolish the inflation", published one month before. The book proposed that the Fixed Abstract Unit became the official currency, and the paper money in circulation worked since then just as redeemable and re-adjustable coupon, no more as currency, once the country's Constitution forbids the existence of two simultaneous moneys. However, the ordinance that released the URV made clear that it was now the currency of the country, but it didn't deprive of this function the Real Cruzeiro, which continued in circulation. There were in practice two moneys, one fixed and abstract, other, re-adjustable and foliar, suffering growing inflationary corrosion, as it already happened before. The advantage, for the population, is that now wages and prices were in URV, abstract, but stable money.

Recognition. Did the population receive the abstract money well?

The ballots that the consumers carried in the pocket were depreciated day after day, but all they knew that these documents were now secondary money, whose losses don't worry more the bearer, since the wages were in strong currency. Many already no more used the concept of Real Cruzeiro, because they transactioned through checks, that now could be written in URV. The president and yours minister of Finance won wide popular recognition, not with the euphoria of the months of the Cruzado Plan, but with the conscience that now a more durable and serene thing was being built. Little by little it was being abandoned the time of the inflationary dry ice, when the value of the money seemed to transform itself in smoke in the face of the proprietor's afflicted glance. This was called by many "inflationary tribute", an expression that didn't reflect the truth, because the loss of the value of the money reached everyone, losing less, it is fact, who possessed more defense mechanisms, as the government and the banks.

The salary earners who could not apply in re-adjustable titles were the largest losers. It was as if, when receiving the wage, half of the ballots fell in a deep well and there it was dissolved. As for the abstract money, it would have been suitable that the old printed money was turned obsolete in the course of time, and this would demand a larger number of months than this that was granted to the population. In October 1994, there would be direct presidential election and a strong point of the campaign would be the release of a printed currency that it turned off the history of the depreciated Real Cruzeiro. With the acquired prestige by having managed the transition for the stable money, Fernando Henrique Cardoso was chosen candidate of the situation, by the Brazilian Social Democracy Party, and the new money was printed in the month of July, under the name Real, with the value of the URV, which was equal to one US dollar, approximately. The candidate, by the effective law, had taken his incompatibility of his position, having been substituted by ambassador Rubens Ricupero, who was who, in fact, released the new currency. The candidate went to palace then to ask the president to allow him to sign the money as Minister of Finance, because this would have great weight in the electoral campaign. The president, man full of ethical sensibilities, didn't find arguments to deny the attendance of the request, but of this he would come complaining hereafter.

Mechanisms. Which were the tools that guaranteed the success of the Real Plan?

An aesthetic innovation in the ballots of the new money was the abandonment of the practice of printing the face of national heroes and other prominent personalities of the Brazilian culture. Instead of politicians, poets, novelists, scientists and military, the honored ones now were animal of forests, seas and rivers, as the jaguar, the macaw, the grouper and the hummingbird. The Real Plan didn't eliminate the inflation, and the Brazilians knew about this, but it removed in an almost definitive way the threat of the hyperinflation. The rates now oscillated below the critical level and the successive governments, starting from 1994, never lowered the guard as for the attendance of the discharge of the prices in the market. Officially, the first mechanism of sustaining of the Real Plan was the safe construction of the process, which involved a transition of ten months. The second mechanism, also official and that was constituted in the great weapon of the Plan, was the deindexation of the economy, what meant the end of the commitments, in all of the contracts, of replacement of inflationary past losses. This was the fatal stroke on the inertial inflation. But the great instrument that gave sustaining to the new currency was the third base, the exchange anchor, guaranteed now no more by purchase and regulation of foreign money, but by the entrance of external capital motivated by the international investors' trust in the new Brazilian economical model. By a suggestion of Simonsen, who was out of the government, but gave orientations to his former students who were part of the economical team of the Ministry of Finance, the value of the Real should overcome that of the dollar. For the Brazilian citizens' surprise, the dollar started to cost 95 cents, later 90 cents and, finally, 83 cents, months after the Real to have been released. Never again the exchange was so valued in Brazil, but this period which the Real was worth more than the dollar brought great happiness to the population, because the imported products, electronic, for instance, were sold with very low prices. The fourth instrument of sustaining of the Real Plan was the use of the interest rate, in agreement with the teachings of the manuals of orthodox economy, what always gives good results in the cases of common inflation, which doesn't depend on pulse fed by noxious capital, but that, in the cases of hyperinflation, or of chronic inflation, only has some usefulness when applied together with other more powerful mechanisms. Finally, the fifth weapon was the daily surveillance, that chilled in the Cruzado Plan and was defeated by the Christmas spirit, but won memorable durability with the Real Plan and became point of honors for all of the governments starting from President Itamar Franco. In short, the base of sustaining of Plano real is composed of the mechanisms of:

(A) transition,
(B) deindexation,
(C) overvaluation,

(D) high interests,

(E) surveillance.

Cost. How did the interest rate become used in the conduction of the Real Plan?

Exchange rate and interest rate, together with the inflation index, form the system of orthogonal axes that represents the integrity of the money. No project of control of inflation can take interest and exchange out of the model. Under regime of inflationary pulse, implementing a plan of sanitation of the money implicates to decide which of the other two communicating vases, interest and exchange, will serve with greater or smaller intensity as blowhole of the pressure which takes firstly, left the market to its own luck, to the warming of the inflation. In normal situation, some disarray of the money that leads to increases in the inflation rate is healed with a well-calculated dose of increase in the interest rates. In the case of chronicle inflation provoked by noxious capital, this strategy of the orthodox economists is not enough, and sometimes it doesn't present result. However, using it together with exchange appreciation can bring good surprises. It is important to discover which interest rate should be practiced as minimum value so that the prices don't get out of the control. That depends less on the trade and more on the power that the Central Bank exercises on the bank system for the establishment of the "spread", the rate indeed practiced by the banks and by the finance companies and that is always larger than the basic official rate, used by the national treasure to pay the interests of its titles and foreign debt. In the first years of the Real Plan, there was many banking systems belonging to the state governments and these acted in consonance with the Central Bank. When the federal government lowered the official interests rate, soon afterwards the federal banks (the fomentation bank, the Federal Savings Bank and the Bank of Brazil) and all of the state banks reviewed this fall for their market interests rates, so that the action of the Central Bank had immediate repercussion close to the consumer. The government came trying to lower the interests for a rate that didn't burden the treasure too much in the service of the debt, but whenever it arrived to a given value, the inflation gave warming signs. Fernando Henrique Cardoso had made to approve amendment to the Constitution that allowed the reelection for one new quadrennial term and the success of the Real Plan guaranteed to him this reelection, but, arriving close of the end of this second mandate, a politics of fall of the interests conducted by the Central Bank had elevated the inflation to preoccupying levels, so that, gradually, the Central Bank tried to elevate the interests to a rate that restrained the increase of the inflation rate. When the time came from giving office to the successor, that by this time was of the opposition, the inflation was practically tamed, but the interests were in the height of the annual 26.5%.

Trust. Did the foreign investors believe in the government begun in 2003?

The new government, of the Workers' Party, vested in January 2003, won the trust of the international markets when, after taking office, showed that it didn't have intention of undoing the previous government's privatizations, nor of beginning innovations in the social area which could go besides the enlargement of politics of benefits cession to poor families, in the program called School-Scholarship, which was ready renamed Family-Scholarship. It was clear for the international investors that the new government was formed by leftist people, but its politics were conservative. Among the parties of the support base, presented with ministries, they was this that before made opposition to the dictatorship of the military ones, the Brazilian Democratic Movement Party, and its rival, which gave sustaining to the dictatorship, the Popular Party, before called National Renovating Alliance. It is emblematic that the party of the dictatorship has adhered in the first hour, while the one of the opposition waited one year to do it. Then the external capitals intensified their entrance in Brazil, at the same time in that the country became a great commercial partner of China in the supplying of agricultural products and ores, to help in the splendid development outbreak verified at that country in the beginning of the 21st century. With the increase of the exports the government accumulated reservations in dollars in the Central Bank in enough amount to pay off the whole volume of the foreign debt, although the national debt continued in strong growth rhythm. The government also paid off the debits with International Monetary Fund (IMF), and he stopped having its economy monitored by the agents of this organ. Little by little, the Central Bank also gave course to a reduction of the basic interests rate, and, of this time, without great frights, because, without the state banks, which had been sold in the previous government's end, the federal banks didn't have a great power for influencing the "spread". In certain hour, the president dismissed the president of the Bank of Brazil, because this didn't come practicing the low "spread" that the government wanted. Far away from being a great problem, this incapacity was a present, because the government could lower the official interests rate and reduce its expenses with the public debt, without putting in risk the inflation rate. The settlements in the economy, allowed by the end of the hyperinflation, take some years to happen, so that Fernando Henrique Cardoso two mandates were difficult. In the government of the Workers' Party the economical growth was re-established and President Luiz Inacio didn't just get to be re-elected, taking office once again in January 2007, but he led the population to choose as president of the Republic the candidate of the Workers' Party, indicated by him, economist Dilma Rousseff, vested in January 2011. On this first year of the new government the basic interests rate was reduced to the range of annual 11%.

Neighboring. How did the neighboring countries in South America live together with this Brazilian saga?

Nobody should have the illusion that the problem of the inflation was solved in South America, because the presidency of the Republic continued installed in the noxious capital, the artificial city of Brasilia, installed at the Brazilian Central Plateau. But, in the same way that Brazil learned how to tame the hyperinflation, also its neighbors made it. Since the application of the Real Plan the annual rates of the Brazilian inflation in the years 1990 were the following ones: in 1994, 1093.8% (half of the year in the Real Cruzeiro and other half in the Real); in 1995, 14.7%; in 1996, 9.3%; in 1997, 7.4%; in 1998, 1.7%; in 1999, 19.9%. In 2011, when it was completing 17 years, the Real accumulated an inflation of 286%. It is a too high rate for every country that lives under consolidated capital, but it gives a normality appearance to an area that got to present inflation annual above 2000%. Brazil occupies half of the territory of South America and its population also reaches approximately half of the South American population. It was not possible to the less powerful neighbors to live without the influence of Brasilia, inclusively implanting military regimes, softer, as the one of Peru, and harder, as the one of Chile and Argentina. This suffocated inflation that Brazil got, it reproduces itself at the neighboring countries. The destiny of Republic of Tutelage, with all of the evils of the demagogy practiced there, is present in all of the Hispanic countries in America, having Brazil as lighthouse. Growths of the GDP distended by the exchange overvaluation should not cause envy to any European country in this beginning millennium. Raised to 6th world economy in the end of 2011, the country, which is the 5th of the world in area and also the 5th in population, iis in the 63rd position in per capita income and in the 84th in HDI (Human Development Index). The European Union should not look for subsidies in the history recent of Brazil to solve the monetary problems caused by the installation of the presidential residence in its secondary capital Brussels.

Turbulence. Is it easy to produce new probation when one leaves an old trouble?

Europe should not repeat the irresistible tendency that Brazil has of fabricating turbulence exactly when it begins to live a good period of bonanza, because this was what happened in 1960 with the abandonment of Rio de Janeiro. In the 17th century Priest Antonio Vieira, who was seminarist in Salvador, returned to Lisbon with many proposals for the court. In his writings he censured the crown for sake of the persecution that it was making against the Portuguese Jews, who, for fleeing of the inquisition, migrated in mass to England and Holland. Expelling the Jews, Vieira said, the government was emptying Portugal of its industrial capacity. By these and other critics, Vieira was arrested by the inquisition in 1666 and, set free after two years, he went to Rome, for doing preaches in Italian. Among Vieira's many suggestions it was one that didn't seem to do sense on that moment: transferring the headquarters of the kingdom to Brazil, so that Portugal could accomplish its destiny of being the fifth empire of the world history. Almost one and a half century later, the idea was accepted, not because the Braganca family had suddenly recognized the pertinence of Vieira's words, but because Napoleon Bonaparte was ready to surround Lisbon with his troops and to depose the dynasty which there reigned, as he had already done with Spain, Naples and several other European crowns. Before the Bonaparte's men came, Dona Maria I, the mad, and its regent son, Dom John, set sail toward Salvador, Bahia, accompanied by about seven thousand of Portuguese and escorted by other thousands of English sailors, there arriving on January 21, 1808. In Bahia Dom John made several decisions that indicated a project of long permanence, or, even, of definitive permanence of the crown in Brazil, which stopped on that year of being colony to transform itself in the larger part of the United Kingdom of Portugal, Brazil and Algarves. He determined that ones brought from Portugal younglets of his favorite fish, sardine, and they spread them in several points of the Brazilian coast. He decreed immediately the opening of the ports to the friendly countries and founded the College of Medicine of Bahia. Salvador had been the capital of the colony up to 1763 and, as Brazil was the largest of the States of the kingdom, coalition of two great territories, which were the State of Maranhao, in the north, and the State of Brazil, in the center-south, is probable that the city soon had conditions to show itself as main capital of this United Kingdom that the regent has just created. As the capital of the colony was in Rio de Janeiro since 45 years ago, government's structures were installed there, and Dom John, alleging commitments already right, transferred months later the headquarters of the kingdom for that city. That didn't work very well, because Dom John, now crowned as Dom John VI, stayed in it few years, returning to Portugal in 1821. The argument was that Bonaparte no longer was threat, and Lisbon, after all, was safe. But the destiny of Brazil would have been other if Rio de Janeiro would be a capital with status. As noxious capital on those times, it only brought insipidities to the monarch, that didn't get, on those thirteen years, to conquer the respect of the cariocas. If we consider that the Brazilians started to recognize Rio de Janeiro in fact as capital in the year of the Independence of Brazil, 1822, then when President Vargas released the currency Cruzeiro, substituting the old Real, of which he cut three zeros, the country had a consolidated capital, healthy, and if the new currency suffered some inflation in the sixteen following years, it was the normal inflation of every civilized economy. In 1958, as it is known, the building of the new capital, Brasilia, was begun. By this time, from 1945 to 1965, Europe passed by intense suffering and heavy diaspora, until the postwar reconstruction came to restore the hope and brought the great phase of progress of the last decades of the 20th century. The European youth didn't live that poverty period, knowing about it by the parents and grandparents' report. The evolution of the human species doesn't have how avoiding the suffering, but it would be much better if we submitted ourselves only to those sufferings due to factors that are out of ours control. One of the more noble objectives of the science is to impede that the humanity produces misfortunes by ignoring the consequences of its actions. And if the proof of an assertive cannot be accepted, or assimilated, even so it is very important that the hypothesis is not despised, when it is matter of avoiding the death and the pain for millions of people. A careful and right decision on the part of the European Council means one relief for the world. To the opposite, a conservative and short attitude, motivated by a difficult position, of the ones that only admit the truths that the mainstream of the academy already consecrated, it will bring the desolation not only for the Europeans, but for all the western world, if not for the whole planet.

4. The reason of the civilizing mission of Europe

From the Europeans the central instrument in the human intelligence appeared.

Roger Bacon: creation of the expression Experimental Science

Newness. Why didn't the European Union notice the danger of doing of Brussels its capital?

It is in number of three the cases of noxious capital. The Europeans are very well forewarned against two of those cases, but no against the third, which only now they experiment in continental terms. The first case, the more evident, is the capital installation in artificial city, as they are the examples of Saint Petersburg and Versailles. The second case is a little subtler, but the Europeans know it of surplus. In this situation, cities that already exist, but that are not great cities, they are transformed in central capitals, as it happened with Madrid and Weimar.

The third and last case is this of Brussels, and it had already happened before, some years ago, without the Europeans to give account. This is why the forecast was made by the Versailles-Weimar Effect's model, but not by the administrators of the European Union. The danger of the installation of the presidential residence in Brussels, for the European Union, it repeats what happened in old Yugoslavia. Marshal Tito, who per decades was ahead of the leadership of State in the city of Belgrade, decided, in his last days of life, to adopt the system of the itinerant capitals. The capitals of the eight federative units would lodge the presidential residence, each during a certain period. In his naive ignorance, this was a way to decentralize the administration and to give the same powers to the several areas of his federation. By that time, the European continent completed 45 years without war occurrences in its territory. It was when, in the action of the abandonment of the healthy capital, Belgrade, the Yugoslavian government began the destruction of the fragile balance of union of those republics. And in little time a war was begun among ethnic groups that shook Balkans during years, leaving a trace of cruelties and genocides that don't find parallel even in the more barbarian tribes of the history. So, the third situation in which one can install a noxious capital was characterized. Then we have the three cases in which the Versailles-Weimar Effect occurs:

    (A) new artificial capital,
    (B) old city transformed in capital and
    (C) secondary capital put as residence of the chief of State.

After all, this last case was what happened to Weimar, which was the capital of the Grand Duchy of Saxe-Weimar before, and also with the city of Hangzhou, but, without the Versailles-Weimar Effect's concept, who could have concluded that this Chinese city would come to be a noxious capital?

Prevention. Is there relationship between the euro crisis and the recent hyperinflation of Zimbabwe?

As we saw, the accumulated knowledge in the several countries gave to the economists the instruments that allow repelling the danger of the hyperinflation. But nor all of the countries are immune. The second largest hyperinflation of the history happened in the 21st century, in Zimbabwe. The international technicians who analyze the situation find a lot of monetarist explanations for the fact, as the confiscation of farms of proprietors of European origin, but the Versailles-Weimar Effect's model could not fail exactly in a case like this. Robert Mugabe built a palace out of the capital, Harare, and in it he established residence. At that time of the construction there were a lot of complaints on the expenses of the work, but this would not have had any great consequence if he had made that palace in the urban area of the capital. Nothing, he decided to build his residence in Borrowdale Brook, rural area 30 km downtown of Harare, to the north, more or less as it was Versailles in relation to Paris. The inflation rate in Zimbabwe in 2007 reached the figure of 66,212.3%, while the annualized rate for 2008, in the month of July, one month before anti-inflationary measures was ordained, it was in 231,150,888.87%. The country's government got to print the ballot with the largest number of zeros in the history: 100 trillion Zimbabwean dollars. Without solution to the view, on April 12, 2009 the government liberated the use of foreign moneys in the domestic transactions, and the population of the country started to use the euro, the dollar of the United States and moneys of neighbor African countries. But the largest first hyperinflation of the history was the one of Hungary, a few after the Second World War: 41,9 quadrillion percent in a month in 1946. What did happen to Budapest, the capital of the country? Simply it had been destroyed in the end of the war. The presidential residence was, by this time, at Lake Balaton. Besides, Hungary was an independent country just since 1918. In the case of the European Union, so big is the knowledge that the great economists have today about the currency that the inflation risk has been left of side: the signs of the crisis reach the service of the debt of the less powerful countries of the block and they have been provoking economical retraction in most of the States-members. Many among them imagine that the European crisis is reflex of the crisis of the credit happened in the United States between 2007 and 2010, but the European Union as a group was free of economical problems until to give office to Mr.

Herman Van Rompuy as first elect President of the block and to install him in Brussels.

Formation. How did occur the settlement of Europe?

The weight of Europe in the humanity's history is so great that a lot of very well educated people think that it invented the civilization. It is not rare to hear somebody to affirm, mistakenly, that Europe created the market, the money and the State. All those items, it is fact, came to America through Europe, which adopted them and improved them. The Homo sapiens of the continent left the Caucasus and dispersed toward the east, the north and the west, but mainly in that direction, where he defeated the Neanderthal man, that reproduced in small amount, and then he established his domain in the whole continental extension at the north of the Mediterranean Sea. When the southern Europeans copied the way of life of Middle East and Asia, they just adapted for themselves the creations of the people that had already invented the cities, millennia before. The wars among city-states produced dispersions of factions defeated by the several habitable areas around Greece and Turkey, leading to the creation of many dispersed principalities along Balkans, the southern Italy and Sicily. The result of the Trojan War led the fugitives to harbor in the surroundings of Rome, if Virgil's Aeneid is not purely imaginative, and on those same years Ulysses, in exploratory trip around the seas during two decades, anchored in the more western area of the coast of the continent and there he founded a new city, which of Ulysses-Polis it became Ulysses-Pol and, finally, Lisbon. This legend doesn't consist of Odyssey, but it is not of all unlikely. If not, which is the legacy of so many years of trip, besides the personal learning?

Legacy. Which was the special present Europe gave to the world?

Besides market, money and State, Middle East and Asia had developed the alphabet and the art of the works, this acted in the practices of the agriculture, the livestock, the cookery, the urbanization, the architecture, the metallurgy, the joinery, the weaving, and so on. All these things the Europeans learned and developed. But in the 7th century BC, the merchant and studious Greek Thales of Miletus brought for the humanity a new way of seeing the world: he invented the science. This speculative science created by Thales cannot be confused with any previous science, because the foregoing erudite men investigated the reality and established relationships among the observed phenomena, as the fact that the stations repeated to each passage of the Earth front to certain constellations, in a period of little more than 360 days, but nobody had demonstrated any of those relationships and, if another made this before Thales, the name was not registered. In every way, very hardly somebody could have made that before the 7th century BC, because the evolutionary conditions of the thought were not ripe. That work of Thales took advantage of the technique of the Geometry, aided by the Arithmetic, instruments used in the Astronomy, which was the other great investigative concern of that businessman. Approximately fifty years later, already in the 6th century BC, Pythagoras of Samos joined the areas of study Geometry, Arithmetic, Astronomy and Music in a great field of scientific investigation which he called Mathematics, name deduced of "mathema", that means "apprenticeship" in Greek. One believes also that he created the word Philosophy, to contain subjects as Ethics, Syllogism, Rhetoric and other. For passing forward to the future generations the knowledge of those two great themes, Mathematics and Philosophy, he created the institution called "school", for forming adolescents and young men in the civilian life, out of the temples and barracks. Before Pythagoras, the boy, on eight or nine years-old, after being instructed in the "paideia", the child's house, which had the function of alphabetizing and was copy of an institution centuries ago used in China, he who was not slave had the options of following military, religious or civil career, but this last one meant to learn some occupation, that transformed him in merchant, artisan, fisherman or any other one which allowed him to win his maintenance when adult. The institution "school"', responsible for a general formation for the civilian life, it was, therefore, a creation of Pythagoras, and this was consequence of the invention of the science (episteme), by Thales of Miletus.

Democracy. From Thales to Socrates, which other important notions did the Greeks develop?

Besides science and school, in the three hundred years that followed other basic creations appeared among the Greeks. Herodotus of Halicarnassus created the Historiography, Hippocrates of Coos formalized the Medicine, out of the arts of the charlatans and the customary healers, and two other great thinkers of that pre-Socratic era released the foundations of two central theories of the contemporary science: the atomic theory, of Physics and Chemistry, and the theory of evolution, of Biology. It was Democritus of Abdera, animated by his master Leucippus, the first researcher to conceive the idea that the matter is formed by very small particles which he called atoms, although, in the modern times the scientists have discovered that those particles are not, as he intended, indivisible. And Anaximander of Miletus, that lived at that time of Thales, saw, wisely, that the live beings had origin in the water, changing, then, and migrating from the rivers and seas for the dry surfaces of the Earth. Today, the theory of evolution, of Lamarck, Wallace and Darwin, is constituted in a great enlargement and in a vast development of that conception, although Darwin admits that he only came to awaken for his creation of the natural selection theory after taking knowledge of the work "An Essay on the Principle of Population", by Thomas Robert Malthus, which describes the fight of the human groups for the survival and presents serious questions concerning the mistakes of the politics in that area. In Athens, the most important of city-states of Greece, it happened the substitution of emperors and tyrants by the chosen ruler in assembly of citizens, with temporary mandates, the elect being by this time able to have his period renewed several consecutive times in the government. There the democracy was born, with Pericles (495 BC to 429 BC) as the most prominent formulator, given that he was re-elect for many terms. As the great ideas always begin incipient, the position for which Pericles was chosen and re-elect was of "demagogue", something that today does to tremble every individual with good prepare in the practice of the citizenship. Obviously, the possibility of countless consecutive reelections by the ruler could not be seen in this phase as harmful thing, as we know today that it is. Being demagogue and being reelect consecutive times, without limitation, as it happened with Pericles in the first decades of the democracy, this represented immense progress before the old destiny of having a tyrant usurper, or even a legitimate emperor, but who didn't have any date to leave the throne while was live. The historian Edward McNeal Burns gives a version a little usual of the meaning of the word "democracy". For him, the word comes from "demos", town, not from "demo", people, and it wanted mean, in the beginning, government of the towns, or of the communities, which sent their representatives to make the political decisions in the assembly. The flourishing of Athens in the century of Pericles, and in the following ones, gives reason to Burns. In a way or other, the important in the democracy idea is that the ruler is chosen by the citizens, for defined terms, and not imposed of Olympus from above and for a lifetime.

Academy. Was really very valuable the legacy of the times of Socrates, Plato and Aristotle?

Plato, who lived from 429 BC to 347 BC, was one of the many youths of Athens who sat down around Socrates to hear his teachings. Pointed out as the more wise man of Greece in a consultation that somebody made to the Oracle of Delphi, it is not of deeming strange that Socrates roused admiration in a large part of the Athenians, at the same time that he provoked envy and hate in another substantial part of that people. One of those furious ones, called Melet, denounced Socrates to the authorities, accusing him of corrupting the young ones, in their faiths and habits. Socrates was not sought by the youths to reaffirm dogmas, but, to the opposite, he had fun in questioning the most ingrained faiths among the Greeks. Why does one have that profusion of gods? Did that make sense? And the boats that stand back in the sea and are going leaving our vision field to what just appears the tip of the mast and, soon then, nor more this? Now, that happens because the Earth is spherical, he taught them. And how about this division between slaves and free citizens? Socrates verified, by experience, that the slaves could understand and learn the theorem of Pythagoras, unlike what the learned citizens thought. Invited by the judges to defend himself of the accusations, he preferred not to do it, because this would mean that he would have to abjure, or then to prove facts that the jurors were unable of understanding. Before this refusal he was condemned to poison himself, drinking a hemlock cup. The episode is described by Plato in the book "Apology of Socrates". Also Plato, in his path, recruited many admirers and many enemies. By writing and speculating about the art of the politics, he had contact with chiefs of State, of the several principalities close of Athens, with the objective of suggesting improvements in the government's conduction. Certain time, at the request of his disciple Dion, he crossed the sea and went to have with emperor Dionysus II, of Syracuse, one of city-states of the Sicily, which was then part of the Magna Greece. Dionysus II, nephew of Dion, was one of the most fearsome tyrants of those times and, instead of thinking about the recommendations of Plato, he got annoyed with the attitude of the Athenian, of going to his palace to do proposals, and ordered his guards to arrest him. Plato then pled to the general Archytas, emperor of the city of Tarentum, who was profiled among his admirers. Archytas of Tarentum, who was in Syracuse, rescued him and led him in turn for Athens. It was known that it was the general Archytas of Tarentum who convinced him of the importance of Geometry. Other ones also tell that it was Archytas who bought and gave as present to Plato the estate in the Garden of Akademos, recommending there he built his school. Akademos was the name of a mythological being, and as the school of Plato was raised there, it started to have the name of Academy. In the three centuries that followed to the death of Pythagoras, happened during the fire that ones provoked at his school, in the south of Italy, an intense debate took place in the Greek cities: Geometry or Music, which of the two was the most important base for science? The experience of the general convinced Plato that the Geometry was the most including and the most useful of the components of science. After all, in it is that Thales made the first demonstrations. Other demonstrations would occur, besides the one of Plato himself. The Academy received studious of the several empires around Athens, certain that the school of Plato was the state of the art in terms of scientific and philosophical knowledge. Among the disciples that Plato received it was Aristotle of Stagira, the son of the doctor of emperor Philip of Macedonia, father of Alexander, future emperor of the world. Aristotle wrote on Ethics, Politics and Aesthetic, but the most important book he delegated us was the "Organon", in that he established the axioms and the basic results of Logic, as a new discipline. If it had not been closed nine centuries later, in the year 529, by emperor Justinian, of Rome, the Academy of Plato would be the university itself today. With 916 years of existence, it was the most durable school in the world to the days today, but, for Justinian, the whole important knowledge was already in the Bible and, like this, we didn't need the school of Plato. The hiatus that was proceeded, of 660 years, made the Academy to return reconstituted in Bologna, in 1189, with a different name: university. But the name "academy" means the idea today generic of university, when used to confront what is inside of it with what is out. We say: "The academy thinks so", or "That is what happens in the academy". Out of Europe, along those first centuries of the Medieval Era inaugurated by Justinian, a type of continuation of the Academy it was installed in the 9th century in Baghdad, by caliph Harun al-Rachid, impelled later by his son and successor al-Mamun, and it was called House of Wisdom. This institution lodged, among other names, poet ibn Haroun, mathematician al-Khowarizmi and translator ibn Qurra, and it worked until the Mongolian invasion, in 1258, when, according to the legend, the books of the House, in its largest part, were thrown in the Tigris River for being used as bridge that allowed the passage of the conquerors' horses. The fall of Baghdad, it is suitable to mark, happened nine years after the final expulsion of the Arabs of the Iberian Peninsula, in 1249, after the five centuries of colonization.

Scholastic. How did Europe escape from the medieval vision of the scholasticism?

The whole investment that had been made in the development of the science in the 6th century, Justinian destined it to the study of the Jurisprudence, what resulted in the making of the "Corpus Juris Civilis", which came becoming the letter of principles for the legislation of the European continent and of Latin America. One can understand the restriction that Plato made to the lawyers as a premonition of what would come to happen to the Academy on those Roman times. In the secondary school, the adolescents studied the curriculum fixed by Boetius, mathematician that was condemned to the death by having criticized Justinian. That curriculum was composed of the *quadrivium* of Pythagoras, with the four fields of Mathematics, and of the *trivium*, formed by Grammar, Rhetoric and Logic. For the study of Philosophy, the youths just had the clergymen's schools. Who wanted formation in Mathematics, he studied a course called "Baccalaureate in Arts", because the idea was not to research, but just to know the technique. The model of the superior studies in the Medieval Era was the Scholastic, theological-philosophical system that tried to reconcile the doctrine of the Catholic Church with the philosophical ideas of Plato. Aristotle was thought as atheist and he was rejected, until Anselm of Canterbury and, after, Thomas of Aquinas overcame the resistances to this reading type and adopted the ideas of the Stagirite in their teaching practice. Among those scholastic teachers, however, the man that deserves larger prominence is one that rebelled against the system itself, criticizing the model of the Scholastic heavily, although servant of it. This man, who stays almost incognito until the days today, was the English friar Roger Bacon, the "Doctor Mirabilis", that lived between 1214 and 1294 and passed great part of life teaching in Paris. From 1277 to 1292 he was arrested in Rome, condemned by the Holy See because of his ideas very ahead of the time. In the book "The First Scientist: a life of Roger Bacon" (2003), Brian Clegg tells that while he wrote the friar's biography and answered to the people the question on whom he was researching, by saying "Roger Bacon", almost always he heard: "Ah, Francis Bacon". He had to explain that this Bacon, Roger, lived three centuries before Lord Francis Bacon and left a very larger legacy. This title of First Scientist Brian Clegg defends that it should be given to Roger Bacon because he created the expression "experimental science" and he worked according to that determination, making scientific experiences. The critic of Bacon to the teaching of the Scholastic came of the fact that it was a school of pure theory. He had knowledge of how the things happened in Baghdad, because he said that the youth of his time to be well formed would needed to dominate three languages: Greek, Latin and Arabic. He described the operation of the telescope, the microscope, the steamship and the balloon of hot air, apparels which would only be created centuries later. He also described the automobile, without many details, but guaranteeing that in the future there would be a car that would move by itself, without traction force of men or horses, and it would reach an enormous speed. He proposed, based on precise calculations, with three centuries of anticipation, the revision of the old Julian calendar for what would be later the Gregorian calendar, of 1582. He also created a new formula for the gunpowder, that Chinese already used, but that the Europeans ignored, and he made a demonstration in public square, lighting one portion of the black powder and provoking great flame. In 1339, 45 years after his death, it had beginning The Hundred Years War, in which the cannons were used thoroughly. Maybe the Englishmen had imagined that, with the use of the gunpowder, they would come to dominate France easily, but what happened, after 116 years of fight, was a situation of exhaustion of Europe and a weakening of defenses that led Constantinople, the oriental Rome, to fall in the hands of the Turks, in 1453, eight years after the end of that conflict. By crooked roads, the medieval world and the Scholastic were extinct, as it was Roger Bacon's dream.

Renaissance. When the Medium Age was finished, were the researchers free for acting?

The decades that followed to the end of the Medium Age consolidated the period of Renaissance, that already was delineated since the times in which Fibonacci introduced the fractions at Padua, Francesco Petrarca created the sonnet, Dante Alighieri wrote his Divine Comedy and other books and Luca Pacioli released the method of the double-entry, in 1494, which became the backbone of Accounting. Pacioli also wrote a book about the "golden ratio", and before the publication he asked Leonardo Da Vinci to illustrate it. As he was friar, he had given to the geometric fact described in the book the name of "divine proportion", and then Da Vinci suggested that he invented a laic name. He proposed that Da Vinci himself took charge of arranging that name, which got being "golden ratio" (the golden point is this that divides a segment in two sections in such a way that the smallest is for the largest as well as the largest is for the size of the whole segment; this division gives the approximate value of .618, and, if we divide the big section by the small, 1.618, number which one uses name with the Greek letter phi). Close to the end of the 15th century Christopher Columbus discovered America and the reports that the Europeans heard on the way of life of the inhabitants of the New World provoked a revolution in the head of the learned men of that time, and then it appeared the era of the Anthropocentrism. In England, Thomas Morus, before releasing the booklet that was fatal to himself on Henry VIII's divorce, he wrote the "Utopia" (1516), a presumed report of a Portuguese navigator about an island whose people lived under an almost perfect social organization. In France, Nicolas Chuquet, François Viète and others developed the use of the letters in the algebra, while Michel of Montaigne wrote, along several years, the 'Essays' (1580), book of reflections on the way of life of the antiquity confronted with the innovations of that time. His youth friend poet Étienne de La Boétie wrote when was an eighteen years old man a small rehearsal against the tyranny, called "Speech of voluntary servitude" (1550). In Italy the youth Galileo Galilei (1564-1642) began the retaking of the scientific researches, in the molds delineated by Roger Bacon, but always with very care, after seeing Giordano Bruno to be burned in the bonfire due to students' accusation on their questions concerning supposed truths of the Bible. Before being Professor of Mathematics in Padua, Galileo would already have been in the history, given that his father, as great enjoyer of Music, made to stage at his home the first opera of all of the times. Galileo enunciated the Law of Pendulum in 1602, what led Christiaan Huygens, in Holland, to develop the pendulum clock (1656). But, even before the Huygens' invent, Galileo can put in practice experiences about speed and acceleration in a way that nobody had gotten before, given that now he could time the minutes and to do more detailed registrations of the movements. It was released then the

Experimental Physics, that would be separating itself of the Mathematics in the middle of the 19th century. Even with all the care of Galileo, he was also denounced and had to abjure before the authorities of the Catholic Church, for having commuted his condemnation to the bonfire for the confinement penalty. Differently of Socrates, who had not how convincing the jurors about his reason truth, Galileo could calmly renounce their statements, because the affirmed facts were to the reach of any person that was not harmed by the dogmatic blindness (four centuries later, pope John Paul II recognized the mistake of the condemnation and rehabilitated Galileo). René Descartes, of France, creator of the Analytical Geometry, when taking knowledge of that sentence, incinerated a volume that was concluding on Optical, fearful that could happen him in the case the text arrived to the clergymen knowledge. It was like this the time of Renaissance in the Europe. The end of the Medium Age, dated officially in 1453, it didn't bring immediately the freedom of thought. There, the outbreak of the truth had to face the threat of the bonfire, brandished by the inquisitors, desperate by seeing that their project of maintaining the continent isolated of the world, under an only and unbreakable interpretation of the reality, was committed.

Differential. How did one reach the creation of the Calculus?

One cannot ignore the paper of the Iberian Peninsula in the rediscovery of science by the renascentist. As a type of nobody's land in the two centuries that followed to the Fall of the Roman Empire, it was invaded by the Moorish Arabs in the year 711. In 732 those invaders also tried to conquer France, but this was more organized and unified, and they were repelled in the Battle of Poitiers, by the Charles Martel's army. Already in the Iberian Peninsula they could settle and stay there for long period. Don Rodrigo Díaz de Vivar (1043-1099) was a nobleman who learned the art of war with those Arab gentlemen, but soon it came him the conscience that having Christian origin would not fit to him to struggle beside the Islamic rulers, however, on the contrary, he should struggle against them. Nicknamed El Cid, or Cid Campeador, of Sid, lord, in Arabic, by being considered lord of war, he showed to the Iberians that it was possible to recover the lands that were in the hands of the Moors. In that time in which the war of reconquest took pulse, an intense intellectual work had beginning in the main Spanish cities. They were the translators, that dominated Arabic and Latin languages and were translating important works of Classical Greece that only existed in Arabic, because the Arabs of Mesopotamia when invading Alexandria rescued of there great amount of books, which passed times after to be studied and reproduced at the House of Wisdom, in Baghdad. Those classic books translated now for Latin was dispersed for other European countries, like England, France and Italian States and they allowed to the masters of that time, even under the restrictive rules of the Scholastic, to reintroduce in Europe the practice of the scientific investigation, which had been utilized, for instance, by the already mentioned Roger Bacon. For sake of those texts preserved by the Arabs, thinkers like Bacon, Galileo, Descartes, Blaise Pascal and Pierre de Fermat became aware of the works of Archimedes, as well as the one of the school of mechanics of Alexandria, in which Ctesibius and Heron took part, and their attempts of developing a mathematical method that allowed to obtain the area of every type of plain figure, i. e., the area under any type of curve, in a search that involved up then the fruitless inquiry of the quadrature of the circle and of the quadrature of the parable. The quadrature of the circle was a type of Saint Graal of the ancient ones and it consisted of finding a method to establish the equivalence between the area of the circle and the area of the square, just using ruler and compass. Archimedes didn't invest a lot in that idea and he preferred to walk on other roads, inventing, to find the area of the circle, the known exhaustion method, that consisted of calculating the area of the regular polygon enrolled in the circumference, refining this polygon so that he had the largest number possible of sides. That method is the embryo of the modern Calculus, of the 17th century. The quadrature of the circle was proven impossible in 1882, for Ferdinand von Lindemann, when showing that the number pi is not algebraic, i. e., it cannot be a root of any polynomial equation of rational coefficients (the number that is not algebraic is a number called "transcendental"), but the quadrature of the parable was solved by Leibniz in 1684, in Germany, through Analytical Geometry. He simply took, for a generic point of the curve, the limit of the ratio formed by the difference of two ordinates upon the difference of the two corresponding abscissas, making this difference of abscissas (delta x) to tend to zero. He perceived that this result was the reduced equation of the straight line tangent to the parable in the considered point. The derived was then invented and, with it, the Differential and Integral Calculus. In this same time, Isaac Newton, in England, had similar concerns, and he discovered also the derived, in an independent way, using, not Analytical Geometry, but Physics. Instead calculating the limit of the difference of the ordinates upon the difference of the abscissas in the parable, he found the limit of the difference of positions in the space upon the difference of the corresponding times, making the difference of times (delta t) to tend to zero. This result equals the instantaneous speed in the considered point. It was the same idea of derived of Leibniz, but with completely different language, so much that, after they enter in communication to discuss those researches, it was long for they notice that they had arrived to the same concept. The integral idea is the one of inverse operation of the derived, and it is that provides the area of those figures that so much took away the sleep of Archimedes.

Applications. Is it easy to understand the use that Keynes made of the derived?

The creation of the Calculus came to bring the solution for many problems that were since many centuries waiting to be resolved. This instrument is used today in areas as varied as Geometry, Astronomy, Meteorology, Statistics, Physics, Chemistry, Engineering and Economics. At the beginning, as it is seen in the writings of Adam Smith and David Hume, for instance, it didn't seem there to be possibility of application of the Calculus to Economics, but the French mathematician Antoine Augustin Cournot (1801-1877) and the English logician William Stanley Jevons (1835-1882) discovered several situations in which the Calculus, mainly the derived, serves very well to the solution of economical problems, and since these days nobody more had doubts that the Economics started to have a new treatment, having a modern and rigorous scientific instrument. It was of this new source that Keynes took the most of his technical results, recognized as unquestionable by Milton Friedman. He used this instrument for elaborating, for instance, the formula of the employment multiplier, deduced starting from the investment multiplier, of his disciple Richard F. Kahn. Everybody knows that, of the common citizens, just a small proportion has some domain of the meaning of Adam Smith's 1776 economical theory. In the case of John Maynard Keynes, it is a small proportion of politicians and economists who have previous foundation to absorb his ideas. Reading the General Theory only once can aid for a first contact with the proposals of the economist of Cambridge, but it is not enough to obtain a clear picture of those innovations of 1936. Unlike what some economists say, the writing of Keynes is not confused. Differently of this, it is very clear and concise. The concepts themselves, those are not elementary and they don't allow immediate intellection.

Difficulty. Is reasonable the critic of Friedman on Keynes?

As bachelor in Mathematics, Friedman didn't have difficulties in digesting the whole group of the technical approach, i. e., of mathematical application, done by Keynes for this discipline that then was called Political Economics. But, to accept the political portion of the General Theory, Friedman would have to open hand of certain precepts that he already fed and this was very silted up in his citizen vision. To justify his rejection to the Keynesian politics, he developed many purely opinionated arguments, for instance, the idea that the preaching of Keynes limited to the economical situation of Great Britain. Happily, such a vision was as an idiosyncrasy of Friedman, an individual position that didn't make important followers. When we compare the most famous economist of the 20th century, Keynes, with the second more famous, Friedman, we need to accept the fact that, once again, Europe was ahead of America. It created science and cultivated it in the best possible way. The other continents are subsidiary and it would not must there to be any question concerning this. The macaroni was created in China and it fits to us to savor it, to improve it in what we can, but not to look for despising the Chinese primacy in this item of the world culture. In the same way, the Aztecs created the eatable corn, this marvel of the cookery, through centuries of experimentation with wild grains, and nobody has motive for wanting to remove from Mexico this important participation in the way of life of the people. We also have to thank to the Phoenician ones, the old inhabitants of the Lebanon, for sake the creation of the phonetic alphabet, improvement of the Egyptian alphabet, which was half phonetic and half ideographic. We have to be thankful to the United States for sake they delegated to the world the jazz and the hydroelectric plant. And to the Indian by they to teach us the practice of the religious fasting, which, even used of laic way, it favors the combat to the obesity and it turns cheap the food for the poor, and also by they to have introduced the representation of zero, in the 9th century, transforming the ciphers in exceptional tool in the development of science and technology. Yes, in the arrival of Columbus to America it was verified that the Mayan ones also had created their representation fore zero, probably in advance, but that of the Indians was already well disseminated in Europe.

America. Is durable the crisis of 2007 in the United States?

The crisis experienced by the United States in 2007 was a crisis of credit. It was not related to the Versailles-Weimar Effect, because its capital is very well consolidated. Today, even the anti-Keynesian economists are unanimous in recognizing as reason of that crisis the problem of the deregulation of the finance market. From August 13, 1971, in the signature of the Richard Nixon's ordinance that abolished the gold standard, until August, 2007, when it came to the surface the problem of the default provoked by the deregulation mechanisms, the followers of the politics of the laissez-faire grew in number and weight in the structures of power of the United States and, little by little, they went eliminating all the mechanisms of defense of the market that were based on the macroeconomics of Keynes. It is not that the United States needed gold standard in that time, but the elimination of that system signaled to government's agents and to the market the contrary of what should do: they thought they were free to reject the monetary and fiscal politics. The privatization of the finance companies of properties, *Freddie Mac* and *Fannie Mae*, had immediate connection with the initial aspects of the crisis, but, even without the Keynesianism, it would have been much soft if two other strong external factors had not served as complicating: the enormous cost of the military occupation of Iraq, initiated in 2003, and the slow and continuous increase of the price of the oil barrel. There is a third external factor of great weight, but this was already foreseen and it was well known of the economists: the market loss in the importer countries for the products manufactured in China, accompanying the accelerated industrial growth of this country. From the years 1980, however, the United States knew that they would have to adapt themselves little by little to this new world configuration and this, even for the men of the *laissez-faire*, could not be reason for abrupt crisis. In the year 2012 the scenery comes with positive perspectives. There is no more the military occupation of Iraq, the sharp picture of unemployment undid itself and the Congress didn't renew the heavy surcharge of several years on import of the ethanol of Brazil. Now, it remains to the North American rulers notice that, to compete with China, preferring the von Mises and Hayek theory against the Keynesian one will mean to brake the economical growth and with this to speed up the arrival of the Asian giant to the position of first world GDP. Anyway, the great crisis of the unemployment in the United States is problem that can be solved with mechanisms supplied by the mainstream of the academy, in period that is not going a lot besides the three or four years. When, however, a country is submitted to the Versailles-Weimar Effect's destructive rigidities, the solution of the several economical problems, as inflation, exchange distortion, high interests, unemployment, public deficit, Brazilization (high inequality), bad education and corruption, it doesn't demand a small number of years, or decades, but it surpasses the period of one century certainly.

Federation. Which the largest political contribution of America?

The great contribution of America to the world is the example of federalism. The League of Delos, the well-known federation experience in the old world, was absorbed by the politics of Pericles and by the success of Athens inside of the Greek culture. The old examples of unification of States, like Persia, Mongolia, China, Alexandre's Hellenic empire and the Roman Empire of the Caesars, they happened in all of the cases starting of the annexation of smaller or weaker empires by a central one. In the Medieval Europe, the Holy Roman-German Empire was dissolved without ever having been implemented, because unification in fact never existed for the constitution of a government organ. And then hundreds of dispersed empires by the territories of Spain, Switzerland, Italy, Germany and Balkans lived together per centuries under the blessings of the papacy. Without Joan of Arc, also the kingdom of the francs would continue divided in a lot of fractions, great part of them dominated by English. The experience of the great federation of States built with success, which was not very evident in its first century, because of the difficulties in the consolidation of the capital, was of fact the one of the United States of America. Under American inspiration, Italian States became unified, to the south, and the Germanic States also became unified, on the north side. The tragic international experience of the First Great War led to the creation of the ephemeral League of the Nations and the Second World War, with its terrible losses in human lives and in material resources, inspired, beside the success of the North American federalism, the formation of the United Nations Organization. However, more important than this, once UN still was not configured as government, the success of the United States raised in the years 1940 the idea of the creation of the federal union of States of Europe. Like this, in 1951 six national States founded the European Coal and Steel Community, and in 1957, through the Treaty of Rome, the European Common Market was formed, what came to give origin to the European Union, created officially in 1992, with the signature of the Treaty of Maastricht, counting then with twelve participant States. In January 2002, the euro, common currency of the most of the countries of the block, it was released as money printed, after experienced since 1999 as scriptural currency. A rigid fiscal discipline was demanded from all of States that adopted the money and this provoked fall in the purchasing power of the populations of the poorest country-members. In October 2007, it was approved the Treaty of Lisbon, that went into effect on January 1, 1999. Among the main decisions of the Treaty were the institution of the position of minister of the external relationships and the position of president of the European Union, to be chosen by the European Council for term of 2.5 years, with possibility of a reelection. The Union itself has much more positive than negative points, and among the advantages of one to build a great federation are these of:

    (A) neutralizing, making obsolete, any separatist guerrilla;
    (B) promoting the free circulation of inhabitants and goods;
    (C) building the fair pride in the federated inhabitants;
    (D) facilitating the mutual protection among States-members;
    (E) creating a great block in the world power's balance.

Presidency. For the population, what is the meaning of the European Union presidency?

When the European Council chose the Belgian former premier Herman Achille Van Rompuy as President of the European Union - officially, President of the European Council -, on November 12, 2009, the block counted with 27 members. Since the times of the European Common Market, the administration of the block was divided among European Commission, working in Brussels, as government, and the rotating presidency, which indicated starting from the first day of every semester the government's leadership of one of the country-members for working as leadership of State. Until Van Rompuy's office, in January 1, 2010, the inhabitants of the European Union didn't see as chief of State somebody that was on the forehead of the whole block, although the institution of the rotating presidency was very much known. For each one, his chief of State was his president or his regional monarch. With the beginning of the validity of the office of European Union president, everything changed in the relationship citizen-government for all of the citizens of the block. The model of popular behavior was now this practiced by the inhabitants of the city in which the President's residence is installed. With Mr. Van Rompuy maintaining the presidential residence in Brussels until May 31, 2012, end of the first mandate, then the European Union completes 2.5 years of financial crisis. If the members of the European Council insist on the same presidential residence, this mandate will just represent one-fortieth of the century of suffering that they will arm to Europe.

Repercussion. Which influence will Brussels have on the Europeans that don't use the euro?

The retraction of the English economy in the end of 2011 sends a clearing message to the leaders of States in difficulty inside of the area of the euro: it does not matter the name of the money inside of the block or around it. If the problem is not solved in the own administration of the block, the only way to escape of the Versailles-Weimar Effect is to put itself under the influence of a country or block, with stability, which has larger power than the one of the original block. An example of this is French Guiana, ultramarine province of France in South America, whose currency never suffered negative influence of the power of Brasilia. Another example was Canada. While the United States lived their difficult decades to consolidate their capital, passing by ethnic massacres, War of Secession, gangsterism and, finally, Great Depression, Canada proceeded free from deeper problems by having its chief of State installed in the Buckingham Palace. By the opposite side, the independent countries that locate in the ray of influence of the country or block that lives under new, or secondary, capital, they suffer disturbances of the same weight or even worst than the influencer country. Mexico, smaller neighbor of States United, passed by stressful revolutionary periods, until finding a demagogic-dictatorial system which turned itself durable, under the direction of the Institutional Revolutionary Party (IRP). Argentina, influenced by Brasilia, suffered in 1976 a military coup d'état led by generals admirer of the Nazism and, in the end of 2001, already rid of the dictatorship of the military ones, it passed by the largest political-economical crisis lived already by a Latin-American country, with a succession of five presidents in only two months. The case of the neighbors from revolutionary Russia was more emblematic.

Russia. Did the retaking of Moscow as capital bring problems to the neighboring countries?

When after the Russian Revolution, of 1917, Lenin, a son of a tsarism's high employee, abandoned Peter the Great's artificial capital, Saint Petersburg (whose first decades had many wars), and returned the government and the leadership of State to Moscow, in 1918, this city had already lost the secular status of capital, since two centuries already it was not used as capital of the country. The conflicts that followed later, as the War of Poland, the Russian Civil War of 1919 and the rebellion of Kronstadt, in 1921, had not only the motivation of the Revolution itself, but also the disarrangement caused by the change of the capital. The following consequences included, first, the fall, as in a domino, of the countries around Russia, that, little by little, weakened themselves and with small autonomy, went being enclosed to that was called Soviet Union, and, second, the implantation of a ferocious dictatorship, under Josef Stalin leadership, soon after Lenin have suffered, in May 1922, the first of the three cerebrovascular accidents which would take him to the death in January 1924. The chiefs of the Council of People's Commissioner that succeeded Lenin, as Rykov, Syrstsov, Molotov and Kamenev, stayed as personalities without expression, without popular recognition concerning their formal positions, given the autocratic power that Stalin was consolidating since 1924. While in the United States the instrument used to do the necessary crossing to the consolidation of the capital was the gold standard, in Russia, the revitalization of Moscow as the supreme leader's residence happened by personal dictatorship. In the beginning of the 21st century the country still seeks to give warranties of continuity to the system of formal democracy, inaugurated in 1989, because the tendency to the relapse in the authoritarianism has been big.

War. Is there relationship between noxious capital and the end of the Austro-Hungarian Empire?

When a chief of State sends his soldiers for an external war, he leaves dismantled his own personal defense. The Russian Revolution happened after three years of disturbances in the military power and in the imperial finances as a consequence of the Russian participation in the First World War. But the more dilapidated imperial power in the episode was this that provoked the conflict: the House of Habsburg. The Austro-Hungarian Empire, the great power of central Europe in the beginning of the 20th century, included from the east of Italy to Ukraine, passing by Croatia, Slovenia, Bosnia-Herzegovina, Serbian, Montenegro, Slovakia, Poland and Romania. Between 1919 and 1939, all of the very informed people from Europe knew that it would happen the World War II. Of the same form, many Europeans knew in the first years of the century that a Great War would come, in date that nobody could know. The murder of the heir of the throne of Habsburg, Archduke Franz Ferdinand, in Sarajevo, that unchained the war, is always counted as a gratuitous action, of a Bosnian activist. Now, who would say? A noxious capital was behind of that crucial event in the world history. Certainly, the Versailles-Weimar Effect's model would be very scratched if it passed over this fact. Emperor Franz Joseph I, as we know, died in 1916 in his Schönbrunn Palace, in Vienna, flanked by Empress Elisabeth. By the rest of the world this did not come to the case, but for the subjects of the Austro-Hungarian Empire the capital in fact was being not the city of Vienna, but Bad Ischl, from at least thirty years ago. If Franz Joseph knew, he would not have died during a period of brutal inflation for his subjects. It would be enough not to have built the Villa Schratt for his concubine Katharina Schratt in Bad Ischl, out of the limits of Vienna. When the heir was murdered, that was a message against an inflationary regime, not a gratuitous act. For the popular understanding, it does not matter where the chief of State stays overnight officially, but where he in fact lives his nights. This place is for the country or for the Union the effective capital, which, when healthy, can make to bloom the progress of the society, and, when noxious, it can bring a world war. Concerning the World War II, it is not necessary to repeat that Weimar engendered the Nazism, by the post-inflation "Savior of the Homeland" effect, and the Nazism was the war itself.

5. The repair in the education

Noxious capital and demagogy are the enemies of the education system.

Maria Montessori: elementary teaching without teacher at the class

Strategy. Is the election of the European Council's President positive fact for the education?

When one is planning the future for the short period, the education system should occupy little or any space of the attentions of the public authorities. But in the strategic planning of long period, or even of medium period, the most basic chapter should be this that deals with the teaching model. The ideas treated here consist already, largely, of other books or articles of this same author, but it is in the present text that the discussion, for the first time, is made taking into account the application of plans in different and varied countries, not just in one only country. For the member States of the European Union, the institution of president's position, elect by the European Council, is something highly promising for the conduction of the education. Such fact, as soon as the problem of the noxiousness of the capital be solved, brings the perspective of neutralization of the demagogic processes that are destroying the education system in several national units. The demagogy itself, the demagogic politicians action, is the largest enemy of the improvement of the teaching, because the politicians tend to see the child firstly as their potential future elector, and, only then, as hope of future development of the country. This behavioral inclination finds antidote in the decision of the Treaty of Lisbon, of doing the choice of the European Council's President of a federative, truly democratic and republican way, without the allure of the popular majority vote, which undermines the representative system and the federation, transforming the politics in championship of commercial perspicacity and leading the big mass to dedicate to the search of the election of the "father of the poor". Happily, with the exception of one or other country that adopt this dark fashion by pure imitation, as it is the case already mentioned of South Korea, only the Islamic and Catholic Republics suffer of this psychopathology.

Dogmas. Which are the wrong beliefs that disturb the current education?

Countries that decide to correct their education systems will only make it if they begin by taking out of the conduction of this work the "modern" bad theoretical ones, who contaminate teachers and school managers with their groundless beliefs. The largest concern has to be with the "modern" because the evils of the traditional education were already denounced broadly in the beginning of the 20th century, and from them few traces still persist. It is important that when choosing a minister of the education the ruler is attentive to do not give office to one of those bad theoretical ones, who defend, among other, the following dogmas:

(1) free-entrance: "tests exclude youth; must be abolished if there are places"

(2) stamp: "tests in general are for stamping the student as obtuse or smart"
(3) decompression: "pressing the student to study leads him to the suicide"
(4) immutability: "school didn't change since Classical Greece"
(5) no-profession: school should teach Language and Mathematics, not Labor"
(6) readiness: "we should not alphabetize child at six y-o, but when he is ready"
(7) right-hand: "Music, Geometric Drawing are not important to the formation"
(8) leveling: "quality doesn't mean differentiation, but complete equalization"
(9) high-cost: "more quality demands greater cost"
(10) no-training: "the basic education should reject the idea of training".

These dogmas try, in the most, to liberate the student of the demand of studies, of the heading for the labor system and of the responsibility of submitting to trainings. Allocating the student autocratically in the subsequent levels of the education system for impeding him of conquering his place through entrance tests it means "to steal" the opportunity of the citizen's development. It is by challenge and by competition that the genius is built in the adolescent, staying latent and atrophic in him when there are no exciting requests. Enough places for all are a great lie, because will not there be ever places for all in Harvard, nor in the wanted high school of the neighborhood. For each one to have the place that wants and that deserves, the fair way is the entrance test, what leads the youth to value the study and to claim one better school, that qualifies him. If the decisive tests are abolished, any playful school that one offers to the boys will be accepted, and they will prefer this to a school that claims them diligence. Concerning the bad theoretical ones, who don't accept trainings, what they don't want is the teaching. For if the school doesn't have how to lead the youths to learning what demand effort and orientation, they can grow, yes, however only in restricted fields. France stops producing new brains as Jules-Henri Poincaré, Irene Joliot-Curie and Pierre-Gilles and begins to present great portions of intellectuals that were formed seating for self-study in their sofas in long and pensive readings, but that have no idea of how one computes partial derived nor of how one processes data of quantum mechanics experiences in laboratory. And they can, ultimately, to repeat the attitude of one of the philosophers of Frankfurt, who wrote diatribes against those who, besides the letters, know the numbers.

Misleading. What mistakes did happen in the passage of the traditional to the modern education?

The old school, previous to the "Casa dei Bambini" (House of Children), of Maria Montessori, founded in 1907, it was sustained in practices that could be accused of "teaching by the trauma", and which were the following ones: (i) physical punishment or spanking in undisciplined or with difficulties student; (ii) demand of memorizing by memorizing ("memorism") as only road for learning; (iii) reduced number of places; (iv) evaluation just in the final of the school year; (v) reprobation by year, in block, even because of a single matter; (vi) absence of rigidity and convention in the mathematical language; (vii) disregard of the student's creative capacity; (viii) fear imposition on the pupil, instead of respect; (ix) separation of students' groups by gender; (x) curricula differentiated for "humanistic" students and "scientific" students. Except a point or another, this system was abolished. But some misunderstandings accompanied that transformation, due, mainly, to the anguish of simply to invert the previous model, without seeking the necessary middle term. Some wrong procedures did have to be eliminated *in totum*, but others would have to be corrected just. It is the case of the "memorism", the demand of memorizing by memorizing. The one that the Montessorian school pointed as mistake was the fact of using the "memorism" as only way to learn a given concept, which did not mean learning, at all, in the most of the cases. Reproducing *ipsis literis* a given sentence was not proof that the student learned the subject and, however, this era the norm. The child shows that he learned the Mathematics of his lessons when he solves the problems and arrives to the expected results, with acceptable writing. He proves that he learned the appropriate Grammar to his series when he writes texts, of his own authorship, without committing serious mistakes of the spelling and syntax part constant of his manuals, or he knows how to recognize morphological classifications and punctuation mistakes when requested to do it in the tests. This student that memorized all of the lessons and does not know how to apply the concepts that were there, he was well poorly educated, and this is what the old school made with the most of the children. What was the misunderstanding committed in the passage of a model to the other? Nevertheless, the learning is only solid when the concepts are assimilated "by heart". The fact of school to leave of demanding "memorism" as only path did not have to mean the satanization of the "memorism" itself. For instance, the student only gets do well the accounts of multiplying and dividing when he knows by heart the times table. The one that changes is that in the modern school this domain is not condition for the child's permanence in the school, because he can assimilate the times table during the years of the elementary school, first triennial, by use and consultation of the material, without taking hits with ruler or punishments by being slower than the friend of the desk at his side.

Reprobation. Is not the larger mistake in the subject of the reprobation?

The case of the students' reprobation in the basic teaching was the point maybe in which the contempt by the search of the middle term caused more damages to the education. The modern purpose of not keeping the student in the grade of the previous year was understood as "*laissez-faire, laissez-passer*", and nothing can be more destructive than this in the formation of the new generations. In the end of the 19th century there were already experiences in relation to the abolition of the reprobation system for series, but until today, in the 21st century, serious mistakes continue to be committed in this area. And it is something too simple to be solved, since the people are dipped in the sense of the middle term. In this case, it just means the following: the student should not be reprobated in the series, for repeating it entirely in the following year, as it happened at the old school, but he should not be released of accomplishing his obligations in the matters in which he showed insufficient learning. This means that if the student of the second grade is going to the third grade with mark 4 in Mathematics and in History, for instance, and the mark to pass in a matter is 5, he has to accomplish during the third grade the relative tasks to those two matters of the second grade, concomitantly to the study of all of the matters of the third grade. Some other further confusions that were done refer to the subject of the annual evaluation and the creativity. Instead of submitting the student to a suffocating week of tests in the end of the school year to decide if he went or not for the following grade, the modern school spread the evaluation by the whole school year, usually with accountancy of the marks bimonthly. Some systems, without understanding the meaning of this change, imposed that evaluations ends could not have decisive role. Now, the healthy model of evaluation is what approves the student that presents good acting in the monthly and bimonthly tests and gives chance to the least agile ones to recover themselves in the end of the school year, in works and tests. If this chance does not exist, those slower students will be promoted by perjury or they will carry their red marks for the following years. The case of the contempt to the creativity, that needed to be corrected, it presents situations today even comic, when students that did not learn anything are approved for showing "creative" solutions, but do not answer to the request of content domain that is presented to them.

Disorder. Which are the new great mistakes of the current school practice?

Beside some or many of those transformation misunderstandings, the current school continues to commit several mistakes that need to be cured so that the children have access to an education system that guarantees them a good formation. Some of those mistakes are the following ones:

(1) lecture - just expositive teaching, without daily exercises for the students;
(2) volatility - study without printed material (books or study aids);
(3) exhaustion - detailing topics too much, without advancing in the contents;
(4) disrespect - elimination of the mechanisms of the teacher's authority;
(5) environment - environment room, without the student to have his room;
(6) super-quiz - week only of proofs, to the end of every bimonthly period;
(7) gap - general tests demanding deferred contents, with incentive to delays;
(8) practicality - tests only with "practical" subjects (that the student didn't live);
(9) electronic - use of cell phone or similar in class (6 to 14 years old);
(10) reinforcement - extra class not for who owes mark, but for studious ones;
(11) skillful - absence of Geometric Drawing, Music and Manual Labors;

(12) pseudo-science - sciences, not Biology (7), Chemistry (8) and Physics (9);
(13) departure - teaching of the departure, without turn (as the division proof);
(14) integral - integral period of regular classes, with teachers;
(15) Taylorism - director that doesn't give classes (out of place Taylorism);
(16) council - bimonthly council of classes, with students, not of annual ones;
(17) adult – short courses for adults, with incentive to the procrastination;
(18) concepts - marks in letters (A, B, C,...), instead of zero to ten;
(19) immobility - difficulty of disturbing students' transfer;
(20) lesion - cerebral atrophies of child without tasks in rooms with 30 or more students.

Those twenty mistakes come to join to the three ones treated already before, which are (a) the authoritarian allocation instead of the qualifying tests of entrance, (b) the free promotion in the matters in which the student did not obtain mark and, finally, (c) the condemnation to the "memorism", since memorizing is the method used by 90% of the students, the sensitive ones, those who do not meet themselves among those that can be called heuristic students. Some of the points need to be detailed. The topic "exhaustion" was treated by Bertrand Russell and concerns teachers who imagine being a good strategy to review subjects by long time, without perceiving, or without wanting to perceive, that when moving forward in the content the themes will be reviewed, in new approach. For instance, when learning division, the student has to revise addition, subtraction and multiplication and, in that fourth operation, yes, he should dedicate a very larger time for the learning. On the "disrespect", it suits to highlight that the tripod of the human progress is formed by the tern "Discipline, Competition and Mobility" (DCM) and, if the teacher does not get discipline in his classes, his work will be fruitless. On the "gap", should be said that the general tests with out of phase contents represent sabotage to the good educational work. The more suitable for the general tests is that they just claim the programmatic content of the grade in issue. For instance, an applied test in the end of the third year of the high school should approach subjects of this grade, not of the previous grades, except as applied resources in the solution of the exercises of the third year. Electronic: use of electronic apparels in children classroom it avails itself of a resource that for the student is magic thing, which does not allow the autonomy of the learning. One should only use instruments that the student can dismount and remount, dominating the process scientifically, what, in the case of electronic apparel, only occurs with youths starting from the sixteen years old. Out of the classroom, differently, the commitment of forming the autonomous and confident citizen does not exist, only this of preparing users and consumers of products, the more mysterious and tantalizing that they are. Integral: regular classes in integral period for the boys of the six to the seventeen years old can result in great accumulation of knowledge in the head of them, but, certainly, it removes them the freedom of growing exercising the learning of the citizen's autonomy, and this contributes to atrophy the creativity. The healthy school supplies one of the periods of the day with regular classes, morning or afternoon, and the counter-period with free activities, without teachers' attendance, having at the most the presence of students' inspectors. In this period without regular classes the student can study, elaborate school works, frequent duties of removing-doubts, play, practice sports, swim, play domino or chess, read books of the library, read magazines or newspapers, see theater, do theater, play drum, play string or blowing instruments, sing in band, sing in choir and, how it is not a room of classes, attend videos. The most appropriate is that for this period the student has another physical atmosphere of school, for instance, an enclosed building, which should be called Center of Studies and Workshops. Taylorism: the separation among administration and commanded ones, that Taylor projected for the efficient operation of factories, it does not have any positive implication when applied to schools and hospitals. The hospitals need to be ruled by doctors or paramedical ones that continue carrying out their origin functions and the school principals should be teachers that maintain their work of giving classes. Being out of this work is losing the key of the conduction of the process. Immobility: the worst attitude of the school administration before a student that surpassed the tolerable limits of the coexistence is not to transfer him of school. For this student, the best lesson is to restart the student life in other school atmosphere, and the worst one is to maintain in the same school unit of the teachers and managers that he disrespected. Lesion: a child without school who grows playing with six or seven friends more, he develops the brain, although without the appropriate learning, but one who maintains locked at room with more than thirty friends, playing, instead of exercising the appropriate tasks to the school learning, this has great chance of atrophying the brain, crystallizing it in the sensorial-motor period of apprenticeship, or in the operative-concrete, because thirty children screaming the whole time one does not give them opportunity to contemplate and to solve problems, even the problems that appear in the games.

Montessori. Is it opportune to retake the proposal of the Montessorian elementary school?

In front of the world crisis of the basic education, it is necessary, finally, to implement what owes to be the modern school. Except the systems of China and, maybe, Finland, what is happening in the several countries of the world is a race for dismantling, which can be described perhaps by a decreasing exponential curve. Therefore it is important that the education systems implement now, after more than one century, the proposal of the "Casa dei Bambini", without reproducing the flaws of the inaugural experience, but introducing, on that new century, mechanisms that save the model invented by Dr. Maria Montessori and, in consequence, save the children learning now. One consolidated the notion that Montessori Method refers to the school use of the didactic materials invented by the Italian doctor, but the nerve center of the Montessorian proposal is the primary teacher's abolition in classroom, fact that the current supposed Montessorian theoretical ones insist in ignoring or outlining, as well as the economists presumed Keynesian look for to ignore that the central proposal of Keynes was the end of the unemployment. Of the four basic three-year periods, for children and adolescents of the six years to the seventeen years old, at least the first three-year period, the Elementary Cycle, which involves the literacy, the reading and the four arithmetic operations, among other initial apprenticeships, it should be treated in the Montessorian way. As is it possible to apply this model in a way that the school is better than the common school? First, (1) each municipal district that decides to enter this model, should begin it in a control group, selecting two or three school units for the change, maintaining the remaining of its net in the precedent system. Second, (2) the teacher is not fired, but just transformed in examiner. Instead of entering the classroom to live together with the children, who will learn how to disobey him and to disrespect him, he works at the teachers' room, or in appropriate places, elaborating tasks for the students and correcting the results. This work is heavier than the traditional, once the reason of being of the child's school life in the Montessorian model is to accomplish learning tasks (we see there that the integral period of regular classes would be something very dark). It is clear that the child should be informed that the execution of those tasks is something entertaining. The exercises of Mathematics, for instance, are naturally games, which the child wins when he goes right. The students do not have to know which teacher prepares or corrects their tasks, because should there not be interaction between teachers and students. Third, (3) the number of students in the classroom is 28 (seven quartets), at the most, and the representative student is this that has obtained the best marks in the first bimonthly period, in the case of the first year, or in the previous year, for the other grades. He is who will be the link between the group and the coordination, bringing to the friends the corrected works, the marks or even the tasks. One of the positive points of the Montessorian system is that the schedule done for a classroom will be the schedule of all of the groups. Fourth, (4) the principal, the coordinator and the students' inspectors, not the teacher, they are the professionals that apply the monthly evaluations in the classroom. The most important evaluation in this first three-year period is the Aloud Reading Test (ART), applied necessarily by the coordinator, who also applies dictations. The writing proof, this yes, can be applied by the other members of the administration. Fifth, (5) the literacy period, in the first two months of the first year, cannot intend the 28 students to dominate the reading with equal self-confidence. Like this, one of the students' inspectors should work as musical animator, who will pass at each classroom of the first year, half hour in each day, in the first month of the school year, to teach ballads of literacy, some alphabetical or numeric, other syllabic ones, which will serve as guide for the children to use the learning material well. With the use of normographic ruler, letters cut out in cardboard and in plastic, times table ruler, pen, rubber, wood materials, pencil and copy-book, the children relate the models and the tasks that they have in hands with the ballads of the musical animator and they reach the literacy quickly, what soon will be checked in the Aloud Reading Test. All the learning is made with letters in lower case and in italic format, which is the middle term between the handwritten letter and the print. The capital letters are deduced quickly after the domain of the reading with the lower cases. Any professional contracted as teacher should be prohibited categorically of exercising the role of musical animator, or of entering the children classroom for any end. Sixth, (6) the students' inspectors accompany, sat in the corridors, the students' work in the classrooms, observing the children through mirrors, conveniently disposed in the entrance of the rooms, as the custom inspectors of the supermarkets make. Seventh, (7) the students' average marks of this Montessorian system should be compared in the end of the school year with the average marks of a group of schools that have been maintained in the previous system and that have been chosen previously in way appropriate for the control. Like this, six schools of very close level are chosen. Three of them start to adopt the Montessorian model and the other three ones continue as before. The tests whose marks come to be used in the comparison should be the same ones, applied in the two groups of schools, by the administrative body of each unit. Two tests can be made in the year for this end, one at the end of the first semester, other at the end of the school year, and those tests are independent of the regular evaluations which will give the marks of the students' progress reports, although they can be used, with some weight, to compose those average marks. With the introduction of the Montessorian method, the student will not have more the classroom teacher, the old versatile teacher, because, when completed the first triennial of the Elementary Cycle, he will have teachers for each discipline. Children formed in the Montessorian way not only will have better conditions to distinguish the deceiving teacher of the good teacher as they will be better prepared to respect their teachers, when finally they have them in classroom. Those teachers, in their turn, will have to be capable to work with wiser and more skilled children, accustomed to solve problems and to give account of their tasks, without spending time with games at the wrong time. The education system needs to avoid that slickers try to confuse the method with retrograde proposed of abolition of essential items to the democratic learning, as grades, physical rooms, uniformed evaluations, written tests, marks, spelling books and textbooks. In the end of the three years, when the first group in the triennial Elementary Cycle is formed, the comparisons of average marks give a picture of which system should prevail. If the work is made without bad will, and without fear, the result will be honest. A substantial advantage for the Montessorian system is an indicative more than enough for the municipal authorities to make the decision of universalizing the model, applying it in the whole net. If, to the opposite, the experience is applied with the whole possible fairness and, even so, the previous system has better acting, what is very little probable, then the Montessorian system should be forgotten, until somebody, in the future, find a new way to apply it with advantages. In all way, a failure in the Montessorian experience will represent the failure in the attempt of educating the people for the autonomy, the discipline and the diligence, with responsibility, what is nothing else that the base of the formation of the human capital that the nations need to build a promising future.

Dilemma. Should the school prepare for the academy or for the job market?

There are many choices in the moment of setting up an appropriate curricular program to the preparation of the students with views to the ends that we judged appropriate in our society. However, the more mentioned dilemma, relative to the options of forming for the academy or for the job market, it is false. Only a biased system school will take a path to the detriment of the other, because the two options are incumbencies that the school system should carry out. If it seeks just the formation for the academy, it will do all those that enter in the education system without the intention of being scientists to feel odd ones out, and the citizens' immense majority is like this. If one does the opposite, worrying just with the preparation for the job market, it denies its origin and its end, and the end of the school system is to form the scientist, even if the most does not want this or do not believe in this destiny. What happens to school is that the scientist is not formed in the first years, but in all of them. The ones that continue in the school seats until the final degree become Full Professor, after being graduated as masters and doctors, who in the United States are called PhD, Philosophic Doctors. The ones that leave school in the first three-year period, or even in the second three-year period, they cannot exercise tasks that demand great sophistication, passing life, in the most of the cases, as workers without qualification. The ones who reach the end of the third three-year period, the Gymnasial Grade or High School Junior (Junior Grade), they can exercise professions a little more complex, as drivers, specialized workers, production inspectors, store cashiers, salespersons, and so on. Who completes the high school level and does not want or does not get to study university, he will have possibility to hug more qualified careers, with the own apprenticeship or by some more months of professional training. Finally, the ones that complete the university exercise the liberal professions or become employees of superior level, reaching perhaps administrators positions. If, with the degree, the university completed, the citizen continues in the academy he will be able to, if he has success in the choice he made, be a scientist. One sees, in this way, that the final objective of school is to form the Full Professor, the searching scientist. As there is not space for all in the academy, this does not mean the school fails in their purposes: it forms the leader. In any degree level, from the Elementary Grade to the university, and even to master's degree, the better prepared by school, in theory, they should be the leaders in their respective environment of performance.

Program. Which should be the curricular program of the courses in the basic teaching?

A curricular program that serves to the purpose of forming for the academy without neglecting of preparing the citizen for the job market, preferably doing him a leader in his area, it needs to have in the Elementary Cycle, for children from six to eight years old, and also in the second three-year period, the Fundamental Grade, for the pre-adolescents from nine to eleven years old, the following configuration, which brings between parentheses the recommended minimum number of weekly hour-classes:

    I. Arithmetic (3);
    II. Geometry (3);
    III. Maternal Language (3);
    IV. History (3);
    V. Geography (2);
    VI. Sciences (2);
    VII. Foreign Language (2);
    VIII. Choir Music (3);
    IX. Artistic Drawing (2);
    X. Citizen Ethic (2).

Here, the subject matter Citizen Ethic is composed by (a) etiquette, (b) rules of traffic, (c) civic duties, (d) principles of jurisprudence, (e) political system, (f) overcoming of the homeland defects and (g) ethical concepts. The third three-year period, for adolescents from twelve to fourteen years old, which is the Gymnasial Grade, or the Junior High School (Junior Grade), should have the following curricular program:

    I. Mathematics (4);
    II. Native Language (4);
    III. Biology, Chemistry and Physics - series 7, 8 and 9, respectively (3);
    IV. History (2);
    V. Geography (2);
    VI. Gymnastics (2);
    VII. Foreign Language (2);
    VIII. Geometric Drawing (2);
    IX. Musical Theory (2);

X. History of the Religion - grade 7 - and Manual Labors - grades 8-9 (2). History of the Religion should be theme provided preferably by the teacher of History, of laic way, approaching several religions, but culminating with the religion of the most in the school unit. The matter cannot be used for proselytism or indoctrinations, and all religious ritual, as well as particular dressing use or cult object, this should be prohibited inside the schools. Religious uniforms, objects and symbols can just be used by the teacher and with purely didactic ends. The subject matter Manual Labors occupies the grade 8 with a chosen modality for the school unit among the options *tailor's workshop, cooking/bakery, horticulture, electricity, printing, joinery* and *locksmithy* (mnemonic: *Tchepjl* system), and the grade 9 with the modality typing/dactylography, common to all of the school units. Manual Labors, Musical Theory and Geometric Drawing develop the ambidextrousy: the basic school cannot be the school of the hand right, which disables the left hand. With the matter Manual Labors the child passes feeling himself useful, discovering the value of their hands, what works for him as therapy against depression, suicidal tendency or other crises of this gender. It develops the necessary manual ability for a future artisan, for one future architect or for a future doctor. It contributes, necessarily, for the formation of a happier and more complete human being. Countries with the matter Manual Labors in the Junior High School have a smaller adolescents' proportion in the juvenile prison systems, in the role of offender minors, likewise being able to close those houses. The accusation of Bolshevism that Friedrich Hayek made against John Dewey because of his proposal of the school Manual Labors is just one more proof that the liberal conservatives are not more than romantic, who judge that the competences and the abilities of the human beings bloom from the nothing, by spontaneous generation. Finally, the Senior High School, Lyceum, or Senior Grade, should have the following matters:

 I. Mathematics (4);
 II. Physics (3);
 III. Chemistry (2);
 IV. Biology (2);
 V. Native Language - grades 10 and 11 - and Latin - grade 12 (4);

VI. Foreign Language (2);
VII. History (2);
VIII. Gymnastics (2);
IX. Psychosocial Technique (2);
X. Operational Technique (2).

The objective of Latin in the grade 12, third year of the Senior Grade, is to serve as rite of passage, besides to provide base for futures studies in Biology, Letters, Philosophy, Laws or History of Science. Since then the youth starts to dominate a language of the educated people, as a prize by arriving to the final year of the basic teaching, differing of the ones that are in the previous grades. The matter "Psychosocial Technique" is composed of History of Philosophy (grade 10), Psychology (grade 11) and Accounting Economy (grade 12). The matter "Operational Technique" is composed by Geometric Drawing (grade 10), Programming of Computers - Excel VBA or another language (grade 11) and Professional Orientation (grade 12). As there is not Geography in the Senior High School, the class of History should use in a lot of occasions the Historical Atlas. The matter Professional Orientation, of the last year of the Senior High School, is composed by ten modalities, having each school unit to choose one of them to offer to its students. This matter should be provided with emphasis in the entrepreneurship. They are the following ones the modalities of Professional Orientation: (1) *organization of events* (by teacher of History, of Drawing, or other), (2) *commercial foreign language for office* (by teacher of Foreign Language), (3) *practical electricity* (by teacher of Physics, of Mathematics, or other), (4) *graphical computation* (by teacher of Mathematics), (5) *clinical analyses* (by teacher of Chemistry, of Biology, or other), (6) *technician-industrial drawing* (by teacher of Mathematics, of Drawing, or other), (7) *architectural drawing* (by teacher of Mathematics, of Drawing, or other), (8) *typing* (by teacher of Maternal Language or other), (9) *administration of human resources* (by teacher of Psychology), (10) *statistical control of quality* (by teacher of Mathematics). The guiding to the professional formation is the best thing that school can offer to its adolescents.

Cares. How should the necessary alterations be discussed in the education system?

Those proposals of curricular programs come from a vision of this beginning of third millennium. In future moments, modifications can be made for adaptation to new demands of the world of the time. Certainly, some matters have universal character and they cannot be removed or substituted, under penalty of offering a school with unforgivable gaps. The parliamentarians that decide to leave their signatures creating and introducing matters they needs to be contained by the regulations of their legislative houses. One item that cannot lack in those regulations is the respect to the principle of the "full disk", which should be worth in relation to school program, public budget and schedule. This means that, as usually there are not spaces to fill out in those pieces, a new item should implicate the exclusion or the shrink of other. Like this, it should be rejected, before entering voting regime, any project of creation of matter in the basic teaching that does not indicate, at the same time, what other matter will be removed or will have its schedule reduced, of way to give space for the entrance of the new one. If the Parliament can make something useful for the curricular programs, this begins by the fixation of the matters in number of ten, as maximum amount, for all the grades of the basic teaching, because a number larger than this will give to the students and the school system the idea that the many contents are not for being taken as serious things. All substitution and all introduction of new contents have to pass by rigorous analysis, because it is not the school itself the base of the social progress, as one imagines, but the quality of the school system, beginning by the discerning choice of the matters, is it. One can build at a country an education system that provides basic and superior education to the totality of its new generations and, even with this, to arm the social and economical disaster. There are models of education systems that are mere wastes of public budgets. In the discussions of some improvement to be done in the system, the larger weight cannot be this of the politicians, but the one of the scientists. The politicians should not alter the education politics without hearing the academy, because the objective of the elementary school is not to prepare little qualified workers, but to initiate the citizen in his walking towards the domain of the science. Those that do not get to be scientists, they should have the necessary preparation to get to accompany the steps of science. In the time of the arrival of the man to the Moon, in 1969, it was noticed that the illiterates, with rare exceptions, were not convinced of the fact. That happened because they did not have the necessary mental preparation for the understanding of the episode, while the educated people, even the one of elementary formation, had the domain of how in general the science and the technology work, what allowed them to assimilate that information.

Improvements. Which new improvements should be implemented at the schools?

Besides the elimination of the mistakes already pointed, the school system needs to take many other measures to give course to the improvement of the teaching. An old discussion concerns the professionals' dispute with the job market of the industries, what leads the teachers of exact sciences, in considerable proportion, to be little time in the teaching. Ones always return with proposals of salary differentiation, with larger remuneration in the hour-class of those teachers. The idea can solve the problem, but at the cost of retrogression, because the fight of the human species has three motivating factors: Survival, Freedom and Isonomy. Systems that have already reached the state of same value for the hour-class to teachers in the same condition of time of work and experience, they should not put it aside. The solution here has to be more meritocratic: teachers of Mathematics, Physics and Chemistry receive certain additional wage if they accept to enroll in a program of special work. In the case of the teachers of Mathematics, this work is the orientation to the school and the co-worker teachers concerning the use of the computers. He can receive, for instance, 25% of the total value of his regular classes as "additional of laboratory", relative to this special work. In the case of the teachers of Physics and Chemistry, this increment occurs by the work in classes of laboratory of their matters. If the payment is monthly, they receive the increment if the month in subject there was work in the laboratory. If it is weekly, they receive if there is the work in the week in subject. The teachers of other disciplines that do not agree to this measure have all the freedom of passing to teach one of those three matters, and the education system will only have to win with this. A second fear that has generated hot debates is this of the payment by good performance. In the case of the basic teaching, with many teachers participating in the student's formation, it is difficult to check who contributed and who disturbed. The attribution of the role of evaluating co-workers teachers is inglorious, since it is impossible. The idea of "good teacher" is individual, each person having a concept of what should be a good professional in the area. A couple of university students discussed in the exit of the class the work of given teacher: for the boy, he was a horrible teacher, who difficultly made to understand; for the girl, he was the best teacher in the university. Since general tests indicate schools with high performance and schools with low one, one can be given financial prizes in the end of the school year to the teachers and servants of those units with high marks, because the professionals' group was shown efficient. But this can never inspire the idea of increasing the teachers' regular wage, even because the high performance can be related to the student type that the school receives, to the participation of the families, and so on. As well as, schools with very low performance in the tests should not be punished with lowering of wages or dismissals, but, to the contrary, they should receive special attention of the General Office of Education, for curing their problems, one of the roads being the relocation of teachers or managers. What is unquestionable quantitatively is the frequency counting of the teachers to the work. And in this case, yes, a fixed percentile can be increased to the educational wage in every month in that he does not commit any lack. This percentile can be 3%, or, if the problem of the absences is very serious, 5%. A third debate is relative to the dispute between private schools and official schools, but it is a subject that does not exist at countries without private school collecting fees. In those in which there is this dispute, it is very common that private schools are sustained by the monthly fees of the children of the official school teachers. If the country admits the competition between official and private systems, it means there is no political restriction to the trade of the teaching. But the distortion provoked by the participation of the women teachers of the official schools (the husbands enter this decision unwillingly) demand a conduction for the subject and it is not other else the concession of bonus-salary to the teachers that maintain their minor children studying in the official system where they give classes. This can be an increment of 3%, if the situation is not very accentuated, or 5%, for the cases in that the contempt to the official school by its teachers largely commits the quality of the teaching. Many other measures should be implemented. *Booklet*: the first book, the spelling one, for the first grades, should be a self-instructive and pleasant book. *Classification*: the teacher's entrance in the career should be by classification in the effectivation test, not by eliminatory mark and the effective teacher should workout in his school unit, not in some preparatory course offered by the teaching net. *Charge*: the teacher's smallest weekly charge of work never should be smaller than twenty classes, except for managers. *Gymnastic*: should be prohibited soccer (addiction) in the regular schedule of classes, Gymnastics being demanded. *Nursery*: infantile education, for zero to six years old children, should be under the responsibility of the General Office of Health, not of the Education, because it is subject for child care, involving breast feeding, motor development, speech therapy, and so on. *Quality*: a new program should not be implanted, but the principles should be followed. *Competition*: one should teach the children the healthy competition (which the romantic ones reject). *Challenge*: Olympiads of Mathematics, entrance tests, contests and comparisons should be implanted, because the challenge creates the genius. *Measurements*: the general national tests starting from the grade 9 should include only four disciplines (Maternal Language, Mathematics, Physics and History) - before this, only Maternal Language and Mathematics. *Prize*: the general tests of gauging should provide prizes to the students of high performance. *Segregation*: by sanctions, one should prohibit the basic school of separating "strong" students' classrooms of "weak" students' classrooms in the same unit. *Relocation*:

teacher or employee badly adapted (not he who gives low marks) should be relocated to another school. *Language*: the musical animator of the first three-year period should teach melodies also in foreign language. *Mark*: the first mark of the Progress Report should be the average of the first three-year period (of twelve bimonthly phases). *Reading*: the first three-year period should be centered in Reading, with contests of Aloud Reading in each school unit. *Rulers*: times table ruler and normographic ruler should be distributed in the first three-year period, recovered at the end of every school year. *Multiplication*: the assimilation of the times table should occur by daily consultation, with veto to the use of the electronic apparels in class. *Regency*: in the schools of basic teaching, managers should give at least two weekly classes.

Numeracy. How to lead the children to value and appreciate Mathematics?

Pythagoras created the word Mathematics as having the sense of "science of the apprenticeship", what means that for him it was the primordial matter in school. In the 20th century Teacher Toru Kumon, after creating his "Kumon Method", resisted for many years to the idea of including any other matter in his work system. After the friends' a lot of insistence, he accepted to introduce the study of languages, which began with Japanese, following, first, by Portuguese, later by Chinese and English. For sake of those friends, he was convinced that just to study Mathematics does not develop all of the students, for great amount of them being necessary to learn before, or at the same time, the language itself, with what they will read and interpret the problems. The consensus that exists today is that Mathematics and Maternal Language form the couple of basic matters, starting from what the student will grow in the other ones. How the child practices Maternal Language's use even when he talks to his friends and to the adults, it is to Mathematics that one needs to dedicate with more insistence, and the school system should emphasize the teaching of Mathematics more than any other. As Bill Gates said, in relation to his children, first it is necessary to learn much Mathematics and English, for later to deal with the computers. For leading the student to value and appreciate Mathematics it is not enough to stop castigating him with the physical punishments of the traditional education and to allow him to consult the times table while he assimilates it. In the old system, he had to memorize it quickly, in order not to receive hit of the teacher, and one of the reasons is that, for the most ones, the education happened in a very short period. One says that Thomas Alva Edison frequented the school for two months, was alphabetized (yes, because two months were enough for this in that time) and, because he was very restless and took hit a lot in class, his mother removed him from there, to complete his education at home, buying him books, demanding him the times table and so on. Even in the cultures in that there is not resistance to the Arithmetic, as what exists in the Iberian nations, the education system needs to work for undoing some myths that disturb the learning of the matter. The great first myth is that an exercise of Mathematics is not something to discuss, and that is done *individually*, always. To break this myth, the education system should implement Olympiads of Mathematics, that happen annually, for students of the third grade and the sixth grade, with a new characteristic: each school unit classifies a team of five students, in each participant grade, and this team makes the tests in group, in the second phase. Who wins the Olympiad in every year is not an individual, but one school unit, through its group of five students, that will work as a team and should win the support and the enthusiasm of the whole school unit. The second myth is also broken with this practice. It gives account that exercises of Mathematics are resolved always *in silence*. The Olympiads in team, however, implicate discussion, so one cannot request silence. The third myth deals with the idea that exercises of Mathematics have *one only way* for its resolution. This comes from the time in that it was only worth what was previously memorized, and the education system needs to break this erroneous precept through orientation to its teachers, who should not accept any resolution that leads to the result, but to accept, yes, every type of resolution that leads to the answer without hurting Logic and without using resources external to the purpose of the subject. Concerning the resistance of Portugal and Spain against numbers, what is only understood when one is transported to the medieval history, time in that the area was colonized by Arabs. It was part of the fight against the Moorish invaders not just the rejection to the Islamic religion, but the several other items of their culture. They were the ones that brought the ciphers, to substitute the Roman numeral ones. Then, for five centuries, this was seen as an aggressive idiosyncrasy of the invader. When they left, after the last battle happened in Portugal in 1249, the rejection to the ciphers stayed in the peninsula, even more than to the Islamism. Offspring ones of Portuguese and Spanish dispersed themselves by the several areas of Europe and by the continents around the world, and they carried for all of the corners this dislike to Arithmetic, inherited by all of the generations since that time. It is not easy to liberate the Iberian children of this inheritance, but something should be made. It should be begun by the explanation that the ciphers are Indian, not Arabic, they having just dispersed the idea around the world. Why not to pass to call them "Indian ciphers", instead of "Arabic ciphers"? And, independently of being called Arabic or Indian, this item that the Arabs brought to the Iberian culture is universal patrimony. Besides everything, the liberation fight ended more than seven hundred years ago.

Reason. What is the reason to give emphasis at this moment to the problem of the education?

Most of the points treated above refer to the life inside the school units. It seems, to the first glance, that the system of the macropolitics is very distant of this, but it is only an impression. School contemplates, at every moment, the structure and the way of being of the national politics and, in the case of blocks, the federative politics. More than this, it prepares the future, much more than the work of the armed forces, the parliaments or the industries. And, in the central politics of the countries or the federations, two horrible negative influences can sabotage all the effort of the education system to form the citizens appropriately: the demagogy of the Republics of Tutelage (Catholic and Islamic), or of ones that imitates them, and the Versailles-Weimar Effect's heavy hand. If the central politics is free from those two unhappinesses, this being the case of China and Canada, it has everything for fomenting and for promoting the growing improvement of the education system. Let us remind, finally, that a country, or block, is politically free and sound when it is not submitted to these vicissitudes:

    (A) noxious capital, by the Versailles-Weimar Effect;
    (B) theocratic regime;
    (C) for life ruler, or a much long-lived;
    (D) demagogy of Republics of Tutelage (direct presidential election);
    (E) pure district voting system.

The sixth error would be the permission to the public servants for maintaining their children in private schools, with paying of fees come of the national treasure, which guarantees their remuneration, but this problem is less dangerous than those other in the short period. For the European Union, the consolidation of the institution of the European Council's presidency drops the perspective of the progress of demagogic politics and this brings great opportunities of growth of the quality of its education systems. But there is this condition: urgent removal of the presidential residence of Brussels, installing it in the healthy capital.

6. Paths for the European Union

It is tragic to deny that the political capital of Europe is the capital of France.

Winston Churchill: proposal of the United States of Europe in 1946

Paris. Which of the European capitals should contain the presidential residence of Europe?

It is very important to emphasize that the healthy capital of a country or block is not necessarily the city of larger economical activity and, as it was already said, it does not need to be the most populous city. New York is the economical-financial center and the most populous city of the United States, but the consolidated capital of the country is Washington-DC, historically, politically and culturally recognized so. Changing the presidential residence for New York would mean to produce more 120 years of sufferings for the Americans, until the new capital to lose the harmfulness. In the European Union the cities of London, Berlin or Rome could be experienced, but there is no need to do great studies to discover that the political capital of the federation in the mental history of the Europeans is Paris. And as it was already mentioned, the great positive point of Versailles-Weimar Effect's model is that it is not necessary to transfer the structure of government for the political capital, but just the chief of State's residence. The administrative capital of the European Union can continue in Brussels, without problems, likewise the Westerner Germany capital was in Bonn until the possibility of the reunification to come. The great negative point is that the cases of validity of the Versailles-Weimar Effect are three:

    A) new artificial city as residence of the chief of State (Versailles - 1709);
    B) old city transformed in political capital (Ravenna - 402);
    C) secondary capital chosen as residence of the chief of State (Nanjing - 1949).

Europeans would neither install a capital in the situation A nor in the situation B, once the historical experiences allow to see and to feel the foolishness of such a decision. But the situation C is not evident and it does not seem taking part of this same list of problems. It would not have been included in the model if marshal Tito had not abandoned Belgrade to try as temporary capitals Sarajevo, Liubliana, Zagreb, Podgorica and Skopje, headquarters of the constituent republics of the federation of Yugoslavia by that time. When he died, in 1980, he left sketched, for the general dissatisfaction, the conditions for the dismemberment of the federation and for the beginning, in April 1992, of the civil war in Bosnia-Herzegovina. For observation of other historical moments, we verified that to install the chief of State's residence in secondary capital is attitude as explosive as to do it in artificial cities like Versailles, in France, or Borrowdale Brook, in Zimbabwe. But let's not forget that the speech of Winston Churchill at Zurich University in September 19, 1946, in which he proposed the creation of the "United States of Europe", recommended as first step in this construction the partnership between France and Germany. The nucleus, thus, of the formation of the great federation would be in Paris or Berlin. Because it has shown its role of consolidated capital more than one time and because it represents the cultural and historical core of the union of the continental people of Europe, the city that should lodge the official residence of the European Council's President is Paris.

Athens. What one can make to revitalize the Greek finances?

Cradle of the civilized Europe, Athens with property has utilized the exploration of the tourism as one of its more fundamental sources of income. The great disadvantage of this economical politics is the dependence of the good financial health of the rich countries. A strong unemployment wave that reaches the United States, Great Britain, Germany and France certainly will provoke fall in the income of countries that have the tourism as element of weight in their national accounts. Of the five countries with larger problems financial in the area of the euro, Greece, Spain, Portugal, Italy and Ireland, the situation of Greece is the most preoccupying, with larger proportion of default families. There are accusations that before the entrance in the area of the euro the financial situation of the country no longer was well, and that manipulations were applied to the balance-sheets, so that the economy seemed to be what it was not. Independently of the truthfulness of this information, it is in relation to Greece that the eyes of the European Commission need to return first. Close to the final of 2011, sociologist George Papandreou gave government's leadership to economist Lucas Papademos, as well as lawyer Silvio Berlusconi resigned in Italy so that President Giorgio Napolitano gave office to Professor Mario Monti, also an economist. Portugal and Spain in the same second semester of 2011 changed their governments, through elections, for prime ministers of conservative liberal parties. Ireland had already made government's change in the first semester. All those member States of the European block are making their financial fittings, always with great dose of orthodox politics. In the Greek case, a politics of the same type can lead to a poverty situation worthy of the pre-emerging countries of continents of the Southern Hemisphere. Besides correct measures of creation of jobs for the less favored classes, the new Greek government, in agreement with the European Commission, needs to revitalize the industry of the tourism, even under the situation of difficulty of the countries that can send visitors for Athens and the Greek islands. Great marketing campaigns should be made, inviting to travel to Greece the middle class of countries as China, Brazil, Russia, India, United States, Canada, Mexico, Germany, France, England, South Africa, Saudi Arabia, Israel, Sweden, Norway, Denmark, Finland, Japan and South Korea, among others. Even if it is small the expense done by visitors of those countries, this will bring a beginning of recomposing of the Greek finances, starting from the incentive to the job.

Several. Which causes are pointed for the crisis of the euro?

The most of the explanations that the economists have been presenting for the financial crisis of the eurozone it blames the currency itself. Among the defenders of the neutrality of the money, the fault is thrown on the leaders who released the unique currency. Among the several attempts of identification of the causes, they are the following ones:

(1) very heavy demands of the euro on the outlying countries;
(2) lack of autonomy of the outlying countries to roll their debts;
(3) loss of the status of emerging countries, with the investors' escape;
(4) end of the ownership of tools to manage the balance of payments;
(5) huge debt of the private sector of Italy and Spain before 2008;
(6) bulky increase of the wages in the south of Europe and in France;
(7) break of the limit rule of 3% of the product for reception of loans.

All these seven explanations indicate problems that would not lead to any crisis if the economical expansion would be guaranteed. If the economy of the United States was in full growth since 2007, this market, together the one of China and other, would guarantee the increase of the product in Europe, and, again, those seven explanations would not work to decipher the origin of the euro crisis. However, if there is a more basic cause, as it is the case of the Versailles-Weimar Effect, any disturbance, easily avoidable in normal situation, will seem an unquestionable cause of the crisis. The worst by-product of this fruitless search of causes is the tendency of blaming people. Many blame the politicians. Others accuse the rich voters by doing pressure on the authorities to impose exaggerating sacrifices to the outlying countries. In the French Revolution Lavoisier, Danton, Louis XVI, Marie Antoinette and Robespierre, among a lot of dozens of politicians and erudite ones, perished in the guillotine. All seemed guilty and they went paying with their own life by this supposed certainty. But the criminal, if there was one, he was in the past: he was Louis XIV, who ordered to build the Palace of Versailles. By this time, the government's chiefs of the five member States in crisis began the year 2011 looking for ways of solving their cash problems, without finding, and they just lost their positions, along the year. Without the euro crisis, they would be well installed in their offices in the beginning of 2012, and their incompetence would not have come to the surface. But Brussels did not give them truces, and it will not give it to any future chief of government for one more century if it insists in lodging the European Council's presidential residence.

Solution. Can be justified the hard measures of Brussels?

Many of the Keynesian economists of the United States minimize the subject of the public deficit in the solution of the unemployment problems. Some get to affirm that the deficit should not be one concern, but they do not take into account that to tolerate deficit and inflation means to give warranties to bad administrators, or incompetent managers. Exaggerated expenses in the government are almost always indication of wrong expenses, therefore, the Keynesian should not give carte blanche to rulers that were already shown relapses, producing deficit in times of good expansion. They should propose that the rulers do investments in the retraction periods, but always demanding that they spend well, because the simple support to the deficit creators can seem a partisan position, not a recommendation sustained in scientific concepts. In the situation of the area of the euro in 2011 and 2012, the influence of Brussels as noxious capital leads to the rulers' squanderer behavior. By becoming capital purely administrative, with the residence of the President of the European Union in Paris, Brussels will be in conditions of fomenting great investments in the member States, favoring the economical growth and the full employment. Before this, the hard orthodox politics seeking the reduction of the deficit and the stopping of the inflation should be accepted, because the opposite is what was in force before. Under Versailles-Weimar Effect and application of orthodox politics, the effective measures are really painful. In order to have not this, and to be in conditions of supplying auspicious politics, we have to live under a healthy capital. We will only then be able to say that the orthodox politics are nonsense, something how to use cannon shot to kill a mosquito.

Invigoration. What positive measures can consolidate the European Union?

If one puts down the euro crisis, accentuated in 2011 with the presidential residence in Brussels, important measures can be taken for the invigoration of the European Union, in way to consolidate it and to place it as one of the three great powers of the world, which are European Union, China and United States. The insistence in the Versailles-Weimar Effect, that comes by the denial of Paris as presidential residence, it can lead the 21st century to repeat the history of the bipolar world, divided in areas of influences of the United States and China, simply. Avoiding this is role of the European Union, which, with administrative capital in Brussels and political capital in Paris, can become every time larger for making the decision of creating:

    I) the Official European Agency of News close to the presidency, in Paris;
    II) the European Scientific University - in Strasbourg;
    III) the European School of Movies and Arts - in Nieuwpoort;
    IV) the Keynesian full employment;
    V) the conditions for the Lingua Franca ("Latino sine flexione", by Prof. Giuseppe Peano, or Interlingua-IALA).

These five institutions should never be used to reinforce the condition of Brussels as residence of the European Council's presidency, how it was done in Brasilia in relation to projects of restoration of Rio de Janeiro, because there is not parallel that one can use to compare the character of certain Brazilian politicians with the European politicians' character. But it is never too much to have the facts on the table. I) This agency is fundamental so that the citizens from Europe, as much of the area of the euro as of out of it, become aware of the installation of the political capital, in way to dismount, the more quickly possible, the Versailles-Weimar Effect's destructive power. II) The project of this institution should seek to the formation of a university that can be compared to the American Harvard and to the English Cambridge. So, it should not collect monthly fees, which should be exempted by the European budget, and its student body should be recruited among the entrant students of the main universities of the European Union, selected the ones that have the largest performance in an test applied to all of them, in a number that varies of ten students, of the less populous member States, to fifty students, of the most populous ones. III) This school of arts is for developing a center for diffusion of the European culture and its classes should be given in English, while this continues as the universal language. IV) The Keynesian full employment is something so simple and essential that can be seen as frightening the fact of it not to be still the norm in the civilized countries. It is the dignifying alternative to the system of public alms of the Law of the Poor, by William Pitt, the Young. The useful work should be the main reason for the existence of employment, but it should not be the only reason. The reason for the employment to exist is that the citizen must have the warranty of sustaining its family. The less qualified workers, or the ones that do not find the wanted places, can have its manpower utilized as in a type of permanent New Deal, in tasks as (a) planting of ornamental trees, (b) painting of trunks of trees, (c) painting of viaducts, (d) aid in the pedestrians' crossing, (e) surveillance of the outside area of schools, (f) counting of cars in the express roads, (g) information of addresses to pedestrians, (h) street arts, (i) measurement of pedestrians' blood pressure, (j) task of giving welcomes to tourists. If nevertheless unemployed people remain, one can apply the proposal of Keynes, hiring a part of that contingent to bury bottles, and other to exhume them the following day, this being before everything an image to inform that the one that matters is the occupation, the elimination of the depressive idleness. Restricting employment in moment of macroeconomic difficulty is pro-crisis politics, and the recommendation of Keynes is that fittings are made in the expansion phases, what led John F. Kennedy to affirm: "The hour of repairing the roof is when the sun is shining". V) The "Latino sine flexione" of Giuseppe Peano can be reconstituted to be the European lingua franca. It is not very different of something as the Italian language itself, but writing with the French spelling, without accent and cedilla, and enriched with the vocabulary of the Spanish language. It can be used in the first years as language of written communication. With the communication lack among the distant people, the languages went distancing themselves along the history, in agreement with the Darwin's speciation principle. Under the means of communication of the present time, it is possible and promising that we revert the process. The successor of Latino Sine Flexione is Interlingua-IALA, by Prof. Alexander Gode, and it can serve better to the purpose of a common language. An alternative to this task, of creating the own language according to the proposal of Peano, is to adopt English as first official language of the European Union, in deference to the maternal languages of the northern part, and Spanish as second official language, which can in little time to be spoken by all the Latin countries of the southern part. In this case, one should have the purpose of doing inside some years all the youths of the Union European to speak the two languages. In any case, the proposal of Peano is better, as well as the one of Alexander Gode, because classic Latin is the base of the speech of Europe.

Validation. How one will subdue the model of the Effect Versailles-Weimar to future tests of validation?

Four cases quoted here of "refuge" of chiefs of State were deducted by the author applying the model of the Effect Versailles-Weimar, being enough next just to investigate for discovering the name of each town: Ravenna (Italy, 476), Bad Ischl (Austria, 1914), Lake Balaton (Hungary, 1946) and Borrowdale Brook (Zimbabwe, 2008). Obvious cases noted along the development of the model were many ones: Aten (Egypt), Byzantium (Oriental Rome), Hangzhou (China), Madrid (Spain), Versailles (France), Weimar (Germany), Saint Petersburg (Russia), Washington (United States), Ankara (Turkey), Crete (Greece), Nanjing (China), Telaviv (Israel), Brasilia (Brazil), Abuja (Nigeria) and Naypyidaw (Myanmar). Since out of the Nazism it is not conceivable to use populations like laboratory, subduing them to situations of stress, the author recommends that the incredulous ones investigate the past history, because countless episodes are still for being explained via the Versailles-Weimar Effect. After knowing the facts here solved, only a totally insane ruler (with syndrome of the Doctor Charbonnet, who inoculated himself with seeds of virus of rabies in the Pasteur's laboratory, for proving that this one was in mistake, but merely serving, with this, of involuntary guinea pig to help Pasteur to develop the anti-rabid vaccine), an irresponsible and sadistic ruler, he will be able to install the leadership of State of his country in secondary capital with the objective of "refuting the theory", being not this country a satellite State. Because it was not with knowledge of cause that Peter I from Russia transferred in 1712 the capital of the Empire to Saint Petersburg, city that he established in 1703. His grandson, Peter II, crowned when he was 12 years old, in 1727, returned, in 1728, the capital for Moscow, but he died of smallpox two years later. The Empress Anna Ivannovna, niece of Peter I, crowned after the precocious death of Peter II, she took of turn to Saint Petersburg in 1732 the residence of the chief of State, who there remained up to 1918, coexisting with economical sorrows, emperors' murders, palatial blows and almost interminable wars with nearby countries. Yes, a refractory future chief of State, who intends to refute the model of the Versailles-Weimar Effect, maybe will come to transfer his residence to a secondary capital and, after provoking the economical disaster, to decree a parallel cause for his bad results. It will not be the first time. Bellow one can see the six greatest hyperinflations in the history, all of them caused by the Versailles-Weimar Effect.

@cacildo
cacildomarques@gmail.com

Read this book in Spanish in the address:
http://cacildo.webs.com/lacrisisdebruselas.pdf

www.ingramcontent.com/pod-product-compliance
Lightning Source LLC
Chambersburg PA
CBHW070147230526
45471CB00002B/554